D1528818

COLOSSIANS
AND PHILEMON

Books in the PREACHING THE WORD Series:

(Unless otherwise indicated, all volumes are by R. Kent Hughes.)

GENESIS:
Beginning and Blessing

EXODUS:
Saved for God's Glory
by Philip Graham Ryken

NUMBERS:
God's Presence in the Wilderness
by Iain M. Duguid

ISAIAH:
God Saves Sinners
by Raymond C. Ortlund, Jr.

JEREMIAH AND LAMENTATIONS:
From Sorrow to Hope
by Philip Graham Ryken

DANIEL:
The Triumph of God's Kingdom
by Rodney D. Stortz

MARK, VOLUME ONE:
Jesus, Servant and Savior

MARK, VOLUME TWO:
Jesus, Servant and Savior

LUKE, VOLUME ONE:
That You May Know the Truth

LUKE, VOLUME TWO:
That You May Know the Truth

JOHN:
That You May Believe

ACTS:
The Church Afire

ROMANS:
Righteousness from Heaven

2 CORINTHIANS:
Power in Weakness

EPHESIANS:
The Mystery of the Body of Christ

COLOSSIANS AND PHILEMON:
The Supremacy of Christ

1 & 2 TIMOTHY AND TITUS:
To Guard the Deposit
by R. Kent Hughes and Bryan Chapell

HEBREWS, VOLUME ONE:
An Anchor for the Soul

HEBREWS, VOLUME TWO:
An Anchor for the Soul

JAMES:
Faith That Works

THE SERMON ON THE MOUNT:
The Message of the Kingdom

PREACHING THE WORD

COLOSSIANS
AND PHILEMON

The Supremacy of Christ

R. Kent Hughes

CROSSWAY BOOKS

A PUBLISHING MINISTRY OF
GOOD NEWS PUBLISHERS
WHEATON, ILLINOIS

220.7
BS8P
v. 51

Colossians and Philemon

Copyright © 1989 by R. Kent Hughes

Published by Crossway Books
        a publishing ministry of Good News Publishers
        1300 Crescent Street
        Wheaton, Illinois 60187

Cover banner: Marge Gieser

First printing, 1989

Printed in the United States of America

Library of Congress Catalog Number 89-50324

ISBN 13: 978-0-89107-488-5
ISBN 10: 0-89107-488-0

Unless otherwise noted, all Bible quotations are taken from *The Holy Bible: New International Version*, copyright © 1978 by the New York International Bible Society. Used by permission of Zondervan Bible Publishers.

RRDC		17	16	15	14	13	12	11	10	09	08	07
17	16	15	14	13	12	11	10	9	8	7	6	5

For
David Hamilton MacDonald,
friend of friends

*"So that in everything
he might have the supremacy."*

(*Colossians 1:18b*)

Table of Contents

Acknowledgments

I must express appreciation to my secretary, Mrs. Sharon Fritz, for her patience and care in typing the manuscripts of these studies; also to Mr. Herb Carlburg for his cheerful, weekly proofreading, and Rev. Jeff Buikema, pastor of Covenant Presbyterian Church, LaCrosse, Wisconsin, for his reading of the manuscript and helpful suggestions. Lastly, special thanks to Dr. Lane Dennis, president of Crossway Books, for his vision for this undertaking and consistent encouragement.

A Word to Those Who Preach the Word

There are times when I am preaching that I have especially sensed the pleasure of God. I usually become aware of it through the unnatural silence. The ever-present coughing ceases and the pews stop creaking, bringing an almost physical quiet to the sanctuary — through which my words sail like arrows. I experience a heightened eloquence, so that the cadence and volume of my voice intensify the truth I am preaching.

There is nothing quite like it — the Holy Spirit filling one's sails, the sense of his pleasure, and the awareness that something is happening among one's hearers. This experience is, of course, not unique, for thousands of preachers have similar experiences, even greater ones.

What has happened when this takes place? How do we account for this sense of his smile? The answer for me has come from the ancient rhetorical categories of *logos, ethos,* and *pathos.*

The first reason for his smile is the *logos* — in terms of preaching, God's Word. This means that as we stand before God's people to proclaim his Word, we have done our homework. We have exegeted the passage, mined the significance of its words in their context, and applied sound hermeneutical principles in interpreting the text so that we understand what its words meant to its hearers. And it means that we have labored long until we can express in a sentence what the theme of the text is — so that our outline springs from the text. Then our preparation will be such that as we preach, we will not be preaching our own thoughts about God's Word, but God's actual Word, his *logos.* This is fundamental to pleasing him in preaching.

The second element in knowing God's smile in preaching is *ethos* — what you are as a person. There is a danger endemic to preaching, which is having your hands and heart cauterized by holy things. Phillips Brooks illustrated it by the analogy of a train conductor who comes to believe that he has been to the places he announces because of his long and loud heralding of them. And that is why Brooks insisted that preaching must be "the bringing of truth through personality." Though we can never *perfectly* embody the truth we preach, we must be subject to it, long for it, and make it as much a part of our ethos as possible. As the Puritan William Ames said: "Next to the Scriptures, nothing makes a sermon more to pierce, than when it comes out of the inward affection of the heart without any affectation." When a preacher's ethos backs up his logos, there will be the pleasure of God.

Last, there is *pathos* — personal passion and conviction. David Hume, the Scottish philosopher and skeptic, was once challenged as he was seen going to hear George Whitefield preach: "I thought you do not believe in the gospel." Hume replied, "I don't, but *he does.*" Just so! When a preacher believes what he preaches, there will be passion. And this belief and requisite passion will know the smile of God.

The pleasure of God is a matter of *logos* (the Word), *ethos* (what you are), and *pathos* (your passion). As you *preach the Word* may you experience his smile — the Holy Spirit in your sails!

R. Kent Hughes
Wheaton, Illinois

1

The Celebration
of the Church

COLOSSIANS 1:1-8

Whell we study Paul's epistles we
see that each has a dominant theme. In Romans, it is justification by faith.
In Ephesians, it is the mystery of Christ and his Church. In Philippians, it
is the joy which Christ brings. In Colossians, it is the absolute supremacy
and sufficiency of Jesus Christ as the Head of all creation and of the
Church. There is no book in the New Testament, including John's Gospel,
which presents such a comprehensive picture of the fullness of Christ.
Accordingly, there is no writing better-equipped to draw us upward than
the book of Colossians.

> Since, then, you have been raised with Christ, set your hearts on
> things above, where Christ is seated at the right hand of God.
> (3:1)

> So then, just as you received Christ Jesus as Lord, continue to
> live in him. (2:6)

As we study Paul's letter to the Colossians, may our view of Christ
be so expanded and permanently impressed on us that we will as a habit
seek those things which are above.

BACKGROUND OF THE EPISTLE

The town of Colosse was located about eighty miles inland from the city of Ephesus, in the Lycus River Valley, in what is today the western part of Turkey. At one time it was one of the prominent towns of the valley, but by the New Testament era it was a small town well in the shadow of its nearby neighbors, Laodicea and Hierapolis. Biblical scholarship believes that the Colossian church came into being during Paul's two-year ministry in Ephesus, because Acts 19:10 says that during that time "all . . . who lived in the province of Asia [which included Colosse] heard the word of the Lord."

The Scriptures reveal that as Paul was preaching in Ephesus, two visitors from Colosse came to believe — namely, Epaphras (4:12) and Philemon (Philemon 19). Philemon later hosted the Colossian church in his home (Philemon 1, 2), and Epaphras served as Paul's lieutenant in evangelizing the Lycus Valley. Thus a new, thriving church sprouted in Colosse though Paul had never been there himself. Paul, of course, had a deep interest in the church and prayerfully advised Epaphras and Philemon as necessary. So it was quite natural that when a major problem arose in Colosse, Epaphras came to him for help.

The problem came from false teachers who were propagating what is called Gnosticism. Gnostics considered themselves to be people of superior knowledge who could help "lesser" Christians attain deeper spirituality. The very word for Gnosticism comes from the Greek word *gnosis*, which means "to know." The Gnostics, "people in the know," the spiritual elite with all the answers, held as their basic doctrine that matter (anything physical or created) was evil and that only the spirit was good. They reasoned, therefore, that God could not be involved in creation, because being perfect he could not touch matter which was intrinsically evil. Therefore, the world came into being through a complicated surrogate process as God put forth thousands of emanations (or lesser gods), each of which was a little more distant from him, so that finally there was an emanation (a little god) so distant from God that it could touch matter — and it created the world. Of course, this lesser god of creation was so far removed from the ultimate God that it was evil.

This reasoning led to the belief that Jesus Christ, if he really was the Son of God, could not have taken on a human body because matter is evil. This delusion spawned the Gnostic romances about Jesus being only a ghost-like phantom. To the Gnostics, Christ was *not* Creator, the Incarnation was *not* real, and Christ was *not* enough!

So the Gnostics built a system by which one could begin with Christ and work one's way up the series of emanations to God. In Colosse, this system (*gnosis*) consisted of ascetic disciplines (many of which were bor-

14

rowed from Jewish legalism, see 2:20-23), secret passwords (borrowed from Eastern mysticism), the esoterica of astrology, and elements of Christianity.[1] It was all very complex and proudly intellectual. The Gnostics, those "in the know," looked down upon the simple Colossian believers, browbeat them, and led some astray.

This is the alarming message which Epaphras brought Paul as he waited in prison. Paul's brilliant response was the Letter to the Colossians, which presented Christ as the Creator and all-sufficient Redeemer in the sublimest terms found anywhere in Scripture. Paul's masterful answer has served the Church well through the centuries as it has repeatedly faced similar heresies and is, in fact, today assaulted by false teachers and cultists who see Christ as only part of the answer.

As we take up Paul's letter, we immediately see that the apostle did not directly attack the Colossian problem, but rather began with an exuberant introduction which celebrated the Colossian church. This was typical of Paul, who characteristically praised the churches before dealing with them pastorally. Paul's heartfelt commendation rose from the miracle which had taken place in Colosse: a poor, pagan people without God and without hope in this world had found Christ. Their lives had been changed, and some remarkable things had happened, which Paul will duly note. His celebration was honest and beautiful, and the celebration is ours as well — for we are the Church.

A CELEBRATION OF JOY (vv. 1, 2)

> Paul, an apostle of Christ Jesus by the will of God, and Timothy our brother, To the holy and faithful brothers in Christ at Colosse: Grace and peace to you from God our Father.

Though Paul had never met the Colossians, he called them "holy and faithful brothers in Christ," which was purposely exalted language. They were God's holy ones, set apart for him. They with Paul shared the same paternity, and they both addressed God intimately as "Abba" (see Galatians 4:6). They shared a mutual domesticity of soul. They were "family," and they naturally called each other brother and sister.

But best of all, they were "in Christ," which is one of the deepest and most joyous of mysteries. In barest terms it means that the Colossians, and indeed all authentic believers, partook of all that Christ had done, all that he was (and is), and all that he ever would be. This is also the essence of the great paragraph with which Paul opened the book of Ephesians. There Paul also defined the Church as being "in Christ" (v. 1), believers whom "God . . . has blessed . . . with every spiritual blessing in Christ" (v. 3), having chosen them "in him before the creation of the world" (v. 4), which resulted in redemption and forgiveness of sins "[i]n him" (v. 7), which in turn eventuated in the hope of glorification "in Christ" and their marking "in him" with the seal of the Holy Spirit. The first fourteen verses of Ephesians use "in Christ" or "in him" no less than ten times to describe the profundity of regeneration in Christ.

As believers, they were "in Christ" and the old had gone, the new had come (2 Corinthians 5:17). Archaeologists tell us that many of the nameless slabs in the catacombs of Rome carried the inscription "*in Christo*" (in Christ), and significantly also bore on the same slab its spiritual corollary "*In pace*" (In peace), testifying to the radical newness and joy which came in Christ.[2] Being in Christ has always been ample reason to celebrate as Paul and the ancient Christians did, and it is the same for us today. This is a wonder of wonders!

We must note that by sealing the above with "Grace and peace to you from God our Father," Paul created a Christian blend of Hebrew and Greek greetings. The customary greeting in the ancient Greek world was *chairen*, which was a form of "grace" and meant "greetings" (see James 1:1; Acts 15:23; 23:26). But in Paul's hands, it became the freshly minted Christian salutation *charis*, "grace."[3] Greeting fellow-believers with this word celebrated the work of grace in their lives. "You are a recipient of God's unmerited favor. Praise God for his grace! This is indeed wonderful!" It was also a commissioning to live under grace.[4] "May you be a great taker. May you have the disposition, the dependency, the humility which makes you a ready receptor of God's grace."

The other half of the greeting, "peace," came originally from the Hebrew *shalom*, which meant more than simply the absence of trouble, but well-being which springs from a sense of the presence of God.[5] Paul's wish for the Colossians was that they would comprehend more fully their peace and enjoy it in all its depth.

It is the same for all people: there must be grace before we experience the *shalom* of God. Grace (God's work) comes before peace (our new relationship).[6] Among the tragedies of our time is humanity's pursuit of personal peace apart from God's enabling grace. That pursuit takes many forms: material, intellectual, social, even religious; but they all end in futility. When sinners find peace through God's grace, that is beautiful, that is cause for rejoicing! "Grace and peace" is the proper Christian greeting and celebration.

A CELEBRATION OF THANKSGIVING (vv. 3-5a)

As Paul continued his greeting, he gratefully made reference to the familiar Christian trio of faith, hope, and love, but placed hope last.

We always thank God, the Father of our Lord Jesus Christ, when we pray for you, because we have heard of your *faith* in Christ Jesus and of the *love* you have for all the saints — the faith and love that spring from the *hope* that is stored up for you in heaven. (vv. 3-5a, emphasis mine)

Faith, hope, and love are mentioned numerous times in Scripture[7] as a sort of "apostolic shorthand" for genuine Christianity.[8] None of these qualities can be manufactured by man; they all come from God.

Paul first celebrated their "*faith* in Christ Jesus." Faith is always mentioned first in the trio because apart from faith there is no Christian experience. Here Paul was very specific about the object of their faith. It was "Christ Jesus." "Everybody needs faith. You gotta have faith," we hear people say. It is considered to be a component of a balanced life — another charm on the bracelet of one's well-being. Having faith means you're okay. But the truth is, faith has no intrinsic value in itself. It must derive its value from its object. When someone says that he or she has faith, the question which must be asked is: "Faith in what? In reincarnation? That God is good? Faith in faith?"

Salvation does not come by believing in belief, or even in a set of doctrines or a creed. Salvation comes by believing in Christ. When John G. Paton was translating the Bible in the Outer Hebrides, he searched for the exact word to translate *believe*. Finally he found it: the word meant "lean your whole weight upon."[9] That is what the Colossians, despite their Gnostic detractors, had done. That was something to celebrate!

Paul then continued to laud the Colossians for "the *love*" they had "for all the saints." For Paul, faith proved its reality by "expressing itself through love" (Galatians 5:6). Loving God is seen in how one loves his neighbor, and particularly another believer (John 13:34, 35). We have all met people who claimed to be good Christians, who were upstanding, honest, and orthodox — but unloving. They had a loveless goodness, an orthodoxy without charity, a questionable faith. They were the kind of people Mark Twain had in mind when he said, "He is a good man — in the worst sort of way." Love for the brethren is a sign of true faith.

When Chuck Colson was serving his prison sentence after the Watergate scandal, his newfound faith was severely tested. His wife did not understand the "born again" business, his son was picked up on drug charges, and Colson himself was despondent. But God met him in his misery. A group of Christians in Washington, including Senators Hatfield, Hughes, and Quie, were praying for him. Senator Quie discovered an old law that allowed an innocent man to serve a prison term for another, and Quie volunteered to serve the remainder of Colson's term.[10] Colson turned him down, but he had experienced "love . . . for all the saints," and Charles Colson was again refreshed in the reality of his faith.

It is a beautiful thing when you see in the Church love for all the saints — not just for some, not just for the lovable, but *all*. This is what made the early church so amazing and so enticing to the ancient world. Barbarian, Scythian, slave and free, male and female, Jew and Greek, learned and ignorant joined hands and sat down at one table. They knew themselves to be all one in Christ Jesus. There never had been anything like it. The world began to babble about sorcery and conspiracies and complicity in unnameable vices. But Christians were only living out their "love . . . for all the saints." A new thing had come into the world — a community held together by love and not by geographical accidents or common language or by the iron chains of the conqueror. The world wondered, and not a few were drawn to Christ. Genuine love for all was cause for Paul's joyous celebration of the apostolic Church, and it is cause for celebration today, for the results are the same.

Finally, Paul celebrated their *hope*: "the hope that is stored up for you in heaven." Hope is placed last because, in this instance, Paul saw faith and love as springing from it.[11] How does hope of Heaven cause faith and love to come forth? As pagans, the Colossians had been without God and without hope in this world. Then came the gospel from Epaphras and Philemon and the wonderful, surprising joy of salvation and hope of Heaven. This joy naturally enlarged their love and faith. This new hope thrust them together as it earned them the natural enmity of the prevailing religious system. In addition, by partaking of the same hope (1 Timothy 1:1), sharing the same secret, they were bound more closely in their love, and thus encouraged greater faith in one another.

How important the hope of glory is! Paul tells us that the hope of the return of Christ and heavenly reward makes a difference in how we live:

For the grace of God that brings salvation has appeared to all men. It teaches us to say "No" to ungodliness and worldly passions, and to live self-controlled, upright and godly lives in this present age, while we wait the blessed hope — the glorious appearing of our great God and Savior, Jesus Christ. (Titus 2:11-13)

John says the same thing:

Dear friends, now we are children of God, and what we will be has not yet been made known. But we know that when he appears, we shall be like him, for we shall see him as he is. Everyone who has this hope in him purifies himself, just as he is pure. (1 John 3:2, 3)

We ought to cultivate our hope. Remember C. S. Lewis's great exhortation?

> Indeed, if we consider the unblushing promises of reward and the staggering nature of the rewards promised in the Gospels, it would seem that Our Lord finds our desires, not too strong, but too weak.[12]

A CELEBRATION OF THE GOSPEL (vv. 5b-8)

The apostle celebrated the gospel's success:

> All over the world this gospel is producing fruit and growing, just as it has been doing among you since the day you heard it and understood God's grace in all its truth. You learned it from Epaphras, our dear fellow servant, who is a faithful minister of Christ on our behalf, and who also told us of your love in the Spirit. (vv. 6-8)

Here Paul engaged in a little justified hyperbole, for though the gospel had not spread "all over the world," it was well on its way. What he was celebrating was its dynamic power and its universality. Unlike the Gnostic elitist foolishness, Christ's Good News was for everybody and was daily reaching new people.

The miracle of the little church in the Lycus Valley was cause for celebration. It is our celebration too, for:
- We are God's holy and faithful ones, saints.
- We are brothers and sisters with a common Father.
- We are "in Christ," and are part of the joyous mystery of his Body.
- The grace of God has been freely poured on us, "grace upon grace" (John 1:16, NASB).
- We have peace, *shalom*, the well-being that results from divine grace and the presence of God.
- God has given us faith, love, and hope: ". . . faith in Christ" — ". . . love . . . for all the saints" — ". . . hope stored up . . . in heaven."

Let us, in joyful continuity with the Colossian church, daily celebrate the Good News of abundance of life in Jesus Christ!

2

The Prayer for the Church

COLOSSIANS 1:9-14

$\mathbf{A}$lmost sixty years ago a young missionary named Raymond Edman staggered in from an Ecuadorian jungle, desperately ill. "He'll be dead by morning," the doctor predicted. Edman's wife dyed her wedding dress black, so it would be ready for the funeral. (In the tropics funerals must be held immediately.) However, thousands of miles away in Boston, Edman's friend, Dr. Joseph Evans, interrupted a prayer meeting, saying, "I feel we must pray for Ray Edman in Ecuador." The group prayed earnestly, until finally Evans called out, "Praise the Lord! The victory is won!" The rest is oft-repeated history: Raymond Edman recovered, his wife's dress did not, and Dr. Edman went on to become president of Wheaton College and to minister for forty years![1] This beautiful story unforgettably affirms the power of intercessory prayer.

Motivated by stories like this, we naturally ask, how are we to pray for the Church, the members of Christ's Body? A classic answer is provided by Paul in the introductory lines of his letter to the Colossians, because they contain his intercession for that distant little church.

In the opening lines of the letter, recorded in verses 1 to 8, Paul celebrated the miracle of this little church's existence in the Lycus Valley. Predictably, this overflowed in prayer, which began in verse 9. His prayer was a beautifully constructed tapestry which makes a perfect model for the fabric of our own prayers. His example tells us how to pray for the *knowledge*, and then for the *conduct*, of the Church.

A PRAYER FOR KNOWLEDGE (v. 9)

For this reason, since the day we heard about you, we have not stopped praying for you and asking God to fill you with the

knowledge of his will through all spiritual wisdom and understanding.

It is significant that Paul prayed for the Colossians' knowledge,
because they were under siege by people who were telling them they
needed a better knowledge, a *gnosis*. The Gnostics were teaching that
Christ was a good place to begin, but that there was so much more they
could know and experience if only they would incorporate the Gnostic
system of passwords, rites, and initiations. Their superior, know-it-all air
was intimidating, and some of the Colossians were made to feel they were
lacking. What is more, the system, by promising a special understanding,
appealed to the people's natural, elitist instinct. And some had fallen. So
Paul's prayer that the Colossians be "fill[ed] . . . with the knowledge of
his will through all spiritual wisdom and understanding" hit the problem
head-on.

This knowledge for which Paul prayed was set in bold contrast with
that of the Gnostics because Paul used a word for knowledge which "is
almost a technical term for the decisive knowledge of God which is
involved in conversion to the Christian faith."[2] The Gnostics' characteristic word for knowledge was *gnosis*. But Paul used the word *epignosis* as a
reference to full knowledge for the Colossians. Knowing that they have
this personal knowledge of Christ and his will, Paul prayed for an *epignosis* which would fill them in such a way that it would instill a wisdom and
understanding which was singularly "spiritual" (the word *spiritual* is
emphatic in the Greek).

From the apostle's perspective, a deep, growing knowledge of
Christ and his will is of the greatest importance to the spiritual life of all
Christians.

And this is my prayer: that your love may abound more and more
in knowledge and depth of insight. (Philippians 1:9)

I pray that you may be active in sharing your faith, so that you
will have a full understanding of every good thing we have in
Christ. (Philemon 6)

I keep asking that the God of our Lord Jesus Christ, the glorious
Father, may give you the Spirit of wisdom and revelation, so that
you may know him better. (Ephesians 1:17)

Here in Paul's Colossian prayer, when he said, "we have not
stopped praying for you and asking God to fill you with the knowledge of

his will," he was using language of great intensity, for he knew that spiritual knowledge is foundational to a sound, fruitful Christian life.³ God puts no premium on ignorance.

Warren Wiersbe says that he once heard a preacher say, "I didn't never go to school. I'm just a igerant Christian, and I'm glad I is!" To which Wiersbe comments, "A man does not have to go to school to gain spiritual intelligence; but neither should he magnify his 'igerance.'"⁴ Spiritual knowledge comes, as we all know, through the work of the Holy Spirit (John 16:8-11). He reveals Jesus Christ and gives us the special saving knowledge of him (John 17:3). But the Holy Spirit does not work alone. The Scriptures become the primary source of "knowledge" for the believer as they are studied in the power of the Holy Spirit. This produces a *Christian mind*, which in fact is what Paul is praying for — a mind, as Harry Blamires says, which is trained to handle life within a framework constructed of Christian presuppositions.⁵ It is this mind, this *epignosis*, which God blesses.

> Blessed is the man . . . [whose] delight is in the law of the Lord, and on his law he meditates day and night. (Psalm 1:1, 2)

> Do not let this Book of the Law depart from your mouth; meditate on it day and night, so that you may be careful to do everything written in it. Then you will be prosperous and successful. (Joshua 1:8)

Typically when we pray for ourselves or for others, we pray for physical health, well-being, social relationships, and spiritual growth. But part of our intercessory prayers ought to be for "the knowledge of his will through all spiritual wisdom and understanding." Have you prayed like this for others? It is an important prayer for your pastor, for new believers, for your family members.

And we ought to be part of the answer to our own prayers! Every believer should be reading and meditating on God's Word. The very blood they bleed ought, in Spurgeon's words, to be "bibline." Every Christian should be concentrating when he or she hears the preaching of God's Word. Every believer should be able to filter his culture's seductive *gnosis* through the grid of God's *epignosis*.

A PRAYER ABOUT CONDUCT (vv. 10-14)

> And we pray this in order that you may live [literally, "walk"] a life worthy of the Lord and may please him in every way. (v. 10)

23

In Hebrew vocabulary throughout the Old Testament Scriptures, the word "walk" symbolically referred to one's conduct, and this carried over into the Greek of the New Testament. For example, in Colossians it is used that way several times:

> . . . that you may walk in a manner worthy of the Lord. (1:10, NASB)

> As you therefore have received Christ Jesus the Lord, so walk in Him. (Colossians 2:6, NASB)

> . . . and in them you also once walked, when you were living in them. (Colossians 3:7, NASB)

In the Hebrew mind, knowledge and conduct were bound together. But in Gnostic culture, teaching was highly speculative and theoretical, not related to life. There was even one school of Gnosticism which reasoned that since the body was evil and the spirit was good, it did not make any difference what one did in the body. So they did anything and everything!

A WORTHY WALK

The Hebrews saw an absolute connection between knowledge and conduct. From their perspective, a person did not know something unless he or she *did* it. This is from where Paul and indeed all authentic Christianity springs. True spiritual knowledge means action! This strikes at the very heart of the unhealthy dichotomy which is so prevalent today. I am speaking of the tendency of people of knowledge not to be activists, and the reverse tendency of people of action to neglect the pursuit of knowledge — thus producing unbalanced extremes.

Let me mention two examples: on the one hand you have the ignorant "soul-winner" who knows only a rabbit track through Scriptures and has no thought-through answers of his own, and on the other hand you have the contemplative scholar filled with knowledge who has never led a soul to Christ. Neither situation was ever meant to be! Paul was the ultimate contemplative mind, but also an incredible man of action. John Calvin, utilizing his transcending intellectual powers, would lie upon his bed and dictate commentaries, but he was also actively involved with people and politics and life. That was also part of the genius of John Wesley, and of Francis Schaeffer in our own day. We need balance.

A profound knowledge should profoundly affect one's walk. It must be understood that any doctrine which isolates the believer from the needs of the world is not a spiritual doctrine. Or put another way, if our doctrine lifts us so high that our feet cannot reach the ground, it is false. Paul prayed that the Colossians would walk their talk, that their knowledge of Christ would grow, and that this in turn would produce a conduct which was worthy of the Lord, pleasing him in all respects. This is how we should pray.

What is to be the result of this worthy walk? "Bearing fruit in every good work" (v. 10). Good works are the outworking of Christ's life in his people. Paul thus prayed that they would act out Christ's kind of life in every situation. Thus the reality of the Colossians' faith would be seen by the surrounding community, and Christ would be glorified and souls drawn to him. The participle "bearing fruit" is present and continuous. Paul prayed that this fruit-bearing would be a constant, ongoing reality.

A KNOWLEDGEABLE WALK

The next thought in Paul's intercession for the Colossians' walk completes verse 10: "growing in the knowledge of God." This is what Paul so powerfully asked for in the beginning of this prayer. Why does he mention it again as he prays for their conduct? Simply because Paul saw the dynamic connection between action and knowledge. He knew that as they continued "bearing fruit in every good work," they would naturally open themselves to "growing in the knowledge of God." One begets the other in a delectable upward spiral: the more one truly serves him, the more one opens to knowledge of him — the more one knows of him, the more one wants to serve. So it goes onward and upward! Jesus himself made it clear that doing the Father's will makes possible the reception of knowledge of the Son (cf. John 7:17). This mutual cause-and-effect relationship between knowing and doing is one of the fundamental laws of spiritual growth. It was one of the secrets of the Wesleyan movement, for John Wesley and his followers did not just find the truth and sit on it — they did the truth! And the doing of it opened them to an increase in the knowledge of God.

A POWERFUL WALK

The next clause which describes Paul's prayer for the Colossians' walk occupies the whole of verse 11:

> . . . being strengthened with all power according to his glorious might so that you may have great endurance and patience . . .

The power which Paul prayed upon the church is immense, for "strengthened" was continuous, denoting a steady supply. And the strengthening is on God's own scale: "according to his glorious might." Colossal power!

The focus of the power is, first, for "endurance." The kind of steadfastness Paul meant is that which "enables one to hold one's position in battle."[6] He had in mind the evil forces in the Lycus Valley which were trying to destroy the Colossian church. Paul was praying that they would stand . . . endure . . . persevere . . . remain steadfast . . . stay at it. Sir Winston Churchill was invited back to his alma mater, Harrow, to address the students near the end of his storied life of public service, which included guiding Britain through her darkest and finest hours. When the five-foot, five-inch bulldog of a man took the platform, everyone waited breathlessly upon his words — and they would never forget what they heard: "Young gentlemen, never give up. Never give up. Never give up! Never! Never! Never!" With that he sat down. Paul would have liked that, especially in regard to the gospel.

To "endurance" Paul added "patience," or as the Greek more literally says, "long-suffering." "Endurance" is in reference to adverse circumstances, whereas "patience" is in reference to difficult people.[7] Paul was praying that the Colossians would have a long-suffering, patient spirit as they related to one another and to those outside the Church. Possessing "endurance" does not mean one will succeed in "patience." Moses endured in his titanic struggle with Pharaoh in Egypt, but his patience with the people failed at Kadesh, and he lost his right to enter the Promised Land (Numbers 20).

> Like a city whose walls are broken down is a man who lacks self-control. (Proverbs 25:28)

How beautiful "endurance" and "patience" are when they are wedded in our life. In 2 Corinthians 6:4-6 Paul listed them as marks of a true minister of Jesus Christ. They perfectly existed in the Lord Jesus himself, who remained steadfast to the end and was long-suffering with all. Paul knew that such qualities could only come by being "strengthened with all power according to his glorious might." This is the way we must pray for our brothers and sisters. "Lord, give them perseverance in difficulties and patience with people. Do it by constantly strengthening them with your power." When King David controlled himself as he was maligned by Shimei, it was a greater victory than his killing Goliath (2 Samuel 16:5-13).

> Better a patient man than a warrior, a man who controls his temper than one who takes a city. (Proverbs 16:32)

The church with "endurance and patience" is a great church. It is a church which walks "worthy of the Lord."

A THANKFUL WALK

How else do we walk worthy? By giving thanks, as verses 11, 12 say: "joyfully giving thanks to the Father." This is the summit of the prayer, and thanksgiving is diffused through all of it. We cannot walk worthy of God without constantly giving joyous thanks, as the Greek participle here emphasizes.

Many years ago Northwestern University had a lifesaving team that assisted passengers on Lake Michigan boats. On September 8, 1860, the *Lady Elgin* foundered near the campus, and a ministerial student named Edward Spencer personally rescued seventeen people. The exposure from that episode permanently damaged his health, and he was unable to continue preparation for the ministry. Some years later when he died, it was noted that not one of the seventeen people he had saved ever came to thank him.[8]

Believers who walk worthy of Christ constantly give thanks to God for their salvation. Why? Paul lists three specific reasons in verses 12 to 14. First, in verse 12 we are to be joyously giving thanks to the Father because he "has qualified you to share in the inheritance of the saints in the kingdom of light." This is a *present* reality (note the aorist tenses). *We are now in the realm of light!*

> For God, who said, "Let light shine out of darkness," made his light shine in our hearts to give us the light of the knowledge of the glory of God in the face of Christ. (2 Corinthians 4:6)

> You are all sons of the light and sons of the day. (1 Thessalonians 5:5)

> But you are a chosen people, a royal priesthood, a holy nation, a people belonging to God, that you may declare the praises of him who called you out of darkness into his wonderful light. (1 Peter 2:9)

We are presently in the light, but it is also a *future* reality! It has not yet been manifested in all its infinite brightness, but we are being made ready for the ultimate inheritance in light. One day we shall pass beyond the stars, and when they have burned themselves out, we will shine even brighter. As C. S. Lewis so memorably put it:

27

Nature. Nature is mortal; we shall outlive her. When all the suns and nebulae have passed away, each one of you will still be alive. Nature is only the image, the symbol; but it is the symbol Scripture invites me to use. We are summoned to pass in through Nature, beyond her, into that splendor which she fitfully reflects.[9]

This is because God the Father "qualified" us for it! It was not due to anything we have done. It is all of him. Thus, we give joyous thanks constantly!

The next reason to give thanks is closely associated with the first. Verse 13 says:

For he has rescued us from the dominion of darkness and brought us into the kingdom of the Son he loves.

The word for "brought" or "transferred" (NASB) is used in other places to describe a mighty king picking up a whole population and deporting it to another realm.[10] That has already been accomplished. All believers have been sublimely deported into "the kingdom of the Son" which, at the Consummation, will be the eternal Kingdom of God (1 Corinthians 15:24).[11] We are in the "kingdom of the Son *he loves*," a Kingdom enveloped in love. For this reason we give joyous thanksgiving.

The final reason for thanksgiving is, as verse 14 says: "in whom we have redemption, the forgiveness of sins." We have been purchased from the slave market, and our sins have been sent away. Why? Because we are in him. That is the *present* reality, right now! And we bow in thanksgiving.

Interceding for other Christians is of greatest importance. Joseph Evans in faraway Boston experienced the urging of the Holy Spirit to lead his congregation to pray for Dr. Edman in Ecuador, and it is my own belief that if he had not followed that urging, Ray Edman would not have lived to minister for the next forty years. When God calls his people to pray and they obey, things happen! When they refuse to follow his urgings, they shorten his sovereign hand.

Why not covenant to pray for both the *knowledge* and *conduct* of your fellow-believers. A church which is growing in the knowledge of Christ and his will, and is walking worthy of him, will do great things. Let us commit ourselves to sensitive, fervent intercession for our brothers and sisters.

3

The Preeminent Christ

Almost a hundred years ago (in 1893), the famous World's Columbian Exposition was held in Chicago, and an astronomical number of people, especially in those pre-automobile days, some twenty-one million, visited the exhibits. America, and particularly Chicago, which had risen phoenix-like from the great fire of 1873, was showing off to the rest of the world. And the show was good. Among the features of the Columbian Exposition was the "World Parliament of Religions," in which representatives of the world's religions met to share their best points and perhaps come up with a new world religion.

D. L. Moody saw this as a great chance for evangelism. Moody commissioned evangelists and assigned them to "preaching posts" throughout the city. He used churches and rented theaters. He even rented a circus tent to preach the Word. Moody's friends wanted him to attack the "Parliament of Religions," but he refused, saying, "I am going to make Jesus Christ so attractive that men will turn to him." D. L. Moody knew that preaching Christ preeminent — the peerless, supreme, all-sufficient Christ, clearly presented — would do the job. And indeed it did. The "Chicago Campaign" of 1893 is considered to be the greatest evangelistic work of Moody's celebrated life, and thousands came to Christ.[1]

Moody's approach was actually nothing new, but rather a time-honored approach which goes all the way back to the apostolic Church and is especially evident in the section of Colossians considered in this chapter. It presented Christ as the One who has first-place in creation and in the Church. The Gnostics had their own version of the "Parliament of Religions" because they considered Jesus to be only one of thousands of emanations from the great unseen God. According to them, Christ was not the way, the truth, and the life (John 14:6), but only the beginning rung in the ladder to the true God.

The Apostolic Church believed otherwise. They believed, to use a cliché, that he is Lord of all, or he is not Lord at all! This is what Paul taught so positively and beautifully here. Verses 15 to 20 are the most closely reasoned presentation of the supremacy of Christ anywhere in the Bible.

CHRIST: SUPREME IN ETERNITY (v. 15a)

The opening line of verse 15 describes Christ as "the image of the invisible God." That God is invisible is a given in both the Old and New Testaments (1 Timothy 1:17; Hebrews 11:27). However, John 1:18, which begins by affirming this, saying, "No one has ever seen God," goes on to say, "God the only Son, who is at the Father's side, has made him known." Jesus is literally the *exegesis* of God. How does he do this? Much of the answer is found in our text as we understand how Christ is the image of God.

The Greek word translated "image" is *eikon*, from which we derive our English word *icon*. This means "an image or representation." Sometimes the Greek word itself meant picture, as when an ancient soldier sent a portrait to his father with the note, "I sent you a little portrait (*eikonion*) of myself painted by Euctemon."[2] From this kind of usage we can say that Jesus is the portrait of God. However, the meaning goes even beyond this because being the *eikon*, the image, of God also carries the idea of revealing the personal character of God. We see this in some of the texts in the Wisdom Literature, such as Proverbs 8:22-31 or the extra-Biblical Wisdom of Solomon 7:24-26, where wisdom was described as the *eikon*, the image or revelation, of God's goodness.[3] Thus, Christ as the "the image of the invisible God" is not just a plaster representation of him, but the revelation of what God is really like.[4] The writer of Hebrews expressed the same thought in very powerful language: "The Son is the radiance of God's glory and the exact representation of his being" (1:3). The Greek word translated "exact representation" here meant the impress left by a die on a coin or a seal on wax. He is the exact impress of the essence of God.[5]

Christ's supremacy in eternity is boldly proclaimed as Paul says he is the *eikon* of the invisible God. *He is supreme!* Jesus is no second-rate emanation from the true God, a Gnostic step in the ladder to the true God. He is God. This not only tells us about Christ — it also tells us about ourselves, because as Jesus is the image of God, he is what we were meant to be in terms of character: we were created in his image (Genesis 1:26, 27).

Jesus is supreme in eternity, and we ought to give him first-place in our lives.

As "image" emphasizes Christ's relationship to the Father, "the firstborn over all creation" introduces his relationship to creation. Here also he is supreme.

CHRIST: SUPREME IN CREATION (vv. 15b-17)

Paul describes Christ's supremacy in creation in four ways in verses 15 to 17. In verse 15b Christ is firstborn; in verse 16 he is Creator; in verse 16b he is the goal; and in verse 17 he is sustainer.

Verse 15b calls Christ "the firstborn over all creation," which at first sight might be taken as teaching that Jesus was the first person created. Indeed the Jehovah's Witnesses, and the heretic Arius long before them, take it this way. But they do so by ignoring the context, which makes him Creator of everything, as well as the rest of New Testament revelation, which makes him eternal (cf. John 1:1). Most of all, they ignore the indisputable fact that while "firstborn" can mean first child, it very often is simply a term which means "first in rank or honor." Sometimes the Torah was called firstborn to indicate its elevated rank. "Firstborn" was a code word for the coming Messiah, as in Psalm 89:27 — "I will also appoint him my firstborn, the most exalted of the kings of the earth." The people of Israel as a whole were sometimes called firstborn to indicate their high position as recipients of the Father's love (Exodus 4:22). So when Paul called Christ "the firstborn over all creation," he meant that highest honor belongs to him. Christ is completely supreme in creation!

Why? Because Christ is Creator. "For by him all things were created: things in heaven and on earth, visible and invisible, whether thrones or powers or rulers or authorities; all things were created by him and for him" (v. 16a). Jesus is the agent of creation *ex nihilo*, from nothing.[6] The extent of his creation is dazzling. It includes even the things in the heavens and the invisible. In fact, it even includes the angels. The Scriptures and Jewish literature reveal that the four descriptions "thrones . . . powers . . . rulers . . . authorities" refer to four classes of angelic powers, with the last two referring to the highest orders of the angelic realm.[7]

The Gnostics taught that Christ was a spiritual emanation from the true God, but here Paul boldly said that he is the true God who created everything, even the invisible spirit-world. *This is an astounding, combative proclamation!*

Christ is Creator of all! We are well aware of what this implies when we think of a universe which is millions of light-years across, but here on our earth it is astounding too. He created even the tiniest creatures. There are 800,000 catalogued insects, with billions in some of the species — all created by Christ.

Christ is not only the Creator of creation, but he is also the end, the goal: "all things were created by him and for him" (v. 16b). This is an astounding statement. Peter O'Brien says, "Paul's teaching about Christ as the goal of all creation . . . finds no parallel in the Jewish wisdom literature or in the rest of the extant Jewish materials for that matter."[8] Some translate the word "for" as *toward*, which makes the sense even more dramatic: "All things were created by him and *toward* him."[9] Everything began with him and will end with him. All things sprang forth at his command, and all things will return to him at his command. He is the beginning and he is the end — the Alpha and Omega. One day everything will give him glory (cf. Philippians 2:11)!

Since this is true, we should live completely for him. Any other course is completely *irrational* for the believer. Paul used similar logic in Romans 11:36 where he said, "For from him and through him and to him are all things. To him be the glory forever! Amen." Then he called us to total commitment, which he concluded was "your reasonable [*logikos*, logical, rational] service" (Romans 12:1, KJV). As a believer, is your life rational or irrational? Are you living totally for God, or are you living outside rationality?

In verse 17, Paul reached the apex of his argument: Christ is superior in creation because he is the sustainer: "He is before all things, and in him all things hold together." The perfect tense here tells us that he continues now to hold all things together, and that apart from his continuous activity, all would disintegrate. The writer of Hebrews puts it this way: "The Son is the radiance of God's glory and the exact representation of his being, sustaining all things by his powerful word" (1:3).

Physicists tell us that among the atom's whirling protons and electrons there is vast space, not unlike our solar system. Though some have theories as to why the atom holds together, none know for sure. Christ is not contained in matter, but he holds it together by his word!

There is a medieval painting which shows Christ in the clouds, and below him the world of humans and nature. From Christ to every object is painted a thin gold thread. The artist was saying that Christ is responsible for sustaining the existence of every created thing.

> *I see His blood upon the rose*
> *And in the stars the glory of His eyes,*
> *His body gleams amid eternal snows,*
> *His tears fall from the skies.*

I see His face in every flower;
  The thunder and the singing of the birds
  Are but His voice — and carven by His power
  Rocks are His written words.

All pathways by His feet are worn,
  His strong heart stirs the ever-beating sea,
  His crown of thorns is twined with every thorn,
  His cross is every tree.[10]

Seeing Christ as he is will keep us from heresy, for it will steel us against a scaled-down Christ which has captured so many lost hearts. And it will cause us to begin to love him with a real love.

Paul's hymn sings of the supremacy of Christ in creation: he is *first-born*, and thus has the highest place. He is *Creator* of everything, every cosmic speck, every spirit. He is the *goal*, and all creation is moving toward him and for him. He is the *sustainer*. He is holding the very breath that falls on these pages. What a stunning revelation this is! It is meant to stretch our puny minds and dominate our thinking and change us. When we truly understand what is being said here, it is amazing that we should ever look anywhere else for meaning and purpose in life. Since he is the Creator who holds all things together, he knows how to best fix and order our lives.

Some years ago a South American company purchased a fine printing press from a firm in the United States. After it had been shipped and completely assembled, the workmen could not get it to operate properly. The most knowledgeable personnel tried to remedy the difficulty and bring it into proper adjustment, but to no avail. Finally the company wired a message to the manufacturer, asking that the company send a representative immediately to fix it. Sensing the urgency of the request, the U.S. firm chose the person who had designed the press. When he arrived on the scene, the South American officials were skeptical — the young man was obviously wet behind the ears. After some discussion, they sent this cable to the manufacturer: "Your man is too young; send a more experienced person." The reply came back: "He made the machine. He can fix it!"

Christ not only created us — he sustains us, and we are made for him. We need to submit our personal problems to him, for he knows how to solve them.

CHRIST: SUPREME IN THE CHURCH (v. 18)

"And he is the head of the body, the church." Christ is sovereign over the Church, just as he is sovereign over creation. When we became believers, we became part of Christ's Body through the baptizing work of the Holy Spirit (1 Corinthians 12:13). "[S]o in Christ we who are many form one body" (Romans 12:5). As members of his Body we are totally dependent upon the Head, Christ, for direction. He is to control us.

The reason for Christ's exalted position in the Church is that "he is the beginning and the firstborn from among the dead" (v. 18). We saw this word "firstborn" in verse 15, where it meant first in rank, and here it means the same thing. Paul was not saying that Jesus was the first person to be raised from the dead, for he was not. However, he was the most important of all who have been raised from the dead, because without his resurrection there could be no resurrection for others (cf. 1 Corinthians 15:20ff.).

Christ chose to enter his own creation, take on a body created and sustained by his power, die, and then undergo resurrection and so be "the firstborn from among the dead" — *and first in rank in salvation*. What a wonder! The Gnostics in all their arcane speculations could never have dreamed up something as stupendous as this. Such a plan, such a dream could only come from the mind of God.

What should this mean to us? Simply this: "that in everything he might have the supremacy" (v. 18). "Everything" extends his "firstness" to as wide a scope as is conceivable and beyond. There is no room for a "Parliament of Religions" here — only Christ preeminent. He must have first-place in everything.

- First-place in our families.
- First-place in our marriages.
- First-place in our professions.
- First-place in our mission and ministry.
- First-place in matters of the intellect.
- First-place in time.
- First-place in love.
- First-place in conversation.
- First-place in pleasures.
- First in eating.
- First in play.
- First in athletics.
- First in what we watch.
- First-place in art.
- First-place in music.
- First-place in worship.

Let us give him first-place!

4

The Supreme Reconciliation

COLOSSIANS 1:19-23

On April 15, 1912, the White Star Liner *Titanic* raised her stern high above the frigid waters of the North Atlantic and began a slow, seemingly calibrated descent as her lighted portholes and towering stern slid silently toward the ocean floor. That famous night saw the extremes of human behavior — from abysmal cowardice to the terrible beauties of sacrificial love. But with the *Titanic* gone and her lifeboats spread upon the icy waters among the crying, drowning swimmers, the story was almost totally devoted to self-serving cowardice, for of the 1,600 people who were not able to get into the lifeboats, only thirteen were picked up by the eighteen half-empty boats that hovered nearby.

In Boat No. 5, when Third Officer Pitman heard the anguished cries, he turned the boat around and shouted, "Now, men, we will pull toward the wreck!" But the passengers protested, "Why should we lose all our lives in a useless attempt to save others from the ship?" Pitman gave in. And for the next hour No. 5, with forty people on board and a capacity of sixty-five, heaved gently on the calm Atlantic, while the forty listened to the fading cries of swimmers 300 yards away. The story was much the same on the other boats. In No. 2, Fourth Officer Boxhall asked the ladies, "Shall we go back?" They said no, so Boat No. 2, about 60 percent full, likewise drifted while her people callously listened. On Boat No. 6, the situation was reversed as the women begged Quartermaster Hitchens to return, but he refused, painting a vivid picture of the drowning over-

35

turning the boat. The women pleaded as the cries grew fewer. Of the eighteen boats, only one boat, No. 14, returned to help — and this was an hour after the *Titanic's* sinking, when the thrashing crowd had "thinned out."[1]

To me, the personal drama of the sinking of the *Titanic* is a parable of a world gone wrong. Fallen humanity is adrift on the unfriendly sea, alienated, unable to help one another despite some furtive individual attempts. The wrongness of everything points to the fundamental problem of people's estrangement from each other and from creation by sin. It is a picture of a world desperately in need of reconciliation and the harmony and rightness which that brings.

Even apart from the terrible story of the *Titanic*, there is no doubt that the world is in need of reconciliation. The inscription on Louis XIV's cannons — *ultima ratio regem* ("the final argument of kings") — is equally descriptive of the mentality of today's rocket-studded world. Man is as profoundly alienated from God now as he has always been since the Fall (see Romans 3:9-18). Indeed, the whole of creation is in desperate need of reconciliation. It is toward this profound need that Paul has been moving us in our study of his letter to the Colossians, and which he now takes up.

THE FATHER'S RECONCILING PLEASURE (vv. 19, 20a)

For God was pleased to have all his fullness dwell in him
[Christ], and through him to reconcile to himself all things,
whether things on earth or things in heaven.

Paul tells us that God the Father found pleasure in having "all his fullness dwell in him" — in Christ. Paul's use of the word "fullness" here was an intentional slap at the Gnostics, who used the same word, *pleroma*, to denote the totality of all the thousands of divine emanations or lesser gods.[2] But Paul said, "No way! Jesus is not one of the lesser gods of the fullness. He is *the* Fullness!" Colossians 2:9 says it even more explicitly: "For in Christ all the fullness of the Deity lives in bodily form." "Fullness" means that the totality of divine power and attributes is in Christ. "The whole fullness — the full fullness" — Jesus Christ is the "exhaustion of God."[3] Moreover, the fullness is said to "live in him." It is not temporary. It was, and is, there to stay.

This means that we need look to no one except Jesus for the full revelation of God's character. If God could only be perceived in closely-reasoned theological language, only the most brilliant could understand him. But the fullness was in Christ, and all we have to do is look at him. As we see him in the Gospels and hear him preached, we can know what God is like.

Secondly, it was God's pleasure "to reconcile to himself all things, whether things on earth or things in heaven" (v. 20a). God means to reconcile creation to himself. Creation suffered a curse because of the Fall (Genesis 3:17, 18). Romans 8:19-22 tells us in sweeping terms that man's sin has subjected the creation to futility:

> The creation waits in eager expectation for the sons of God to be revealed. For the creation was subjected to frustration, not by its own choice, but by the will of the one who subjected it, in hope that the creation itself will be liberated from its bondage to decay and brought into the glorious freedom of the children of God. We know that the whole creation has been groaning as in the pains of childbirth right up to the present time.

This is more than poetry. Creation actually does moan, but it will be brought back to its primal obedience — like it was before the Fall. That is why we sing at Christmas:

> *No more let sins and sorrow grow,*
> *Nor thorns infest the ground;*
> *He comes to make his blessings flow*
> *Far as the curse is found.*

The land and seas will lose their hostility! Everything in the universe will be reconciled except that which rejects him — which brings up the main focus of this verse: the reconciliation of sinners to himself. In every reference to reconciliation between God and man in the New Testament, it is God who takes the initiative (see Ephesians 2:16, which uses the same word as here; also the verbs in Romans 5:10 and 2 Corinthians 5:18-20 and the nouns in Romans 5:11 and 11:15 and 2 Corinthians 5:18, 19). Reconciliation to God is an explicitly one-sided process! He does virtually everything. All we have to do is respond.

What we should note here is that "God was pleased" to have the fullness dwell in Jesus and through him to reconcile us. Salvation is God's joyous work. What an inviting revelation to a lost world!

THE FATHER'S RECONCILING METHOD (vv. 20b, 22a)

The Father's method of reconciliation is seen in two parallel clauses from verses 20 and 22: "making peace through his blood, shed on the cross"; "But now he has reconciled you by Christ's physical body through death." God's method is the death of Christ.

It is said that years ago in a western city a husband and wife became estranged and chose to separate. They moved away and lived in different parts of the country. The husband happened to return to the city on a matter of business and went out to the cemetery to the grave of their only son. He was standing by the grave in fond reminiscence when he heard a step behind him. Turning, he saw his estranged wife. The initial impulse of both was to turn away. But they had a commonhearted interest in that grave, and instead of turning away they clasped hands over the grave of their son and were reconciled. They were reconciled by death![4]

Our personal reconciliation took nothing less than the death of God's Son; but his death and its effects went far beyond any human death.

> God was reconciling the world to himself in Christ, not counting men's sins against them. And he has committed to us the message of reconciliation . . . God made him who had no sin to be sin for us, so that in him we might become the righteousness of God. (2 Corinthians 5:19, 21)

Jesus bore the separation of sin so reconciliation could take place. He made "peace through his blood, shed on the cross" (v. 20). "[H}e himself is our peace" (Ephesians 2:14). As Dorothy Sayers put it, "Whatever the answer to the problem of evil, this much is true: God took His own medicine." The Cross is the ultimate evidence that there is no length the love of God will refuse to go in effecting reconciliation.

> He who did not spare his own Son, but gave him up for us all — how will he not also, along with him, graciously give us all things? (Romans 8:32)

It is *God's pleasure* to give you all things. Have you responded to him?

THE FATHER'S RECONCILING PURPOSE (vv. 21, 22)

> Once you were alienated from God and were enemies in your minds because of your evil behavior. But now he has reconciled you by Christ's physical body through death to present you holy in his sight, without blemish and free from accusation.

God's purpose rises from mankind's miserable condition. In the original, "alienated" was an unusually powerful word which indicated a persistent and permanent condition.[5] This continuous alienation from God expressed itself in a mind that was hostile to him and eventuated in evil deeds. This is the way all people are without Christ, but humanity doesn't like to hear it.

When a great seventeenth-century Christian woman and encourager of God's servants, Lady Huntingdon, invited one of her friends, the Duchess of Buckingham, to hear George Whitefield preach, she received this reply:

> . . . It is monstrous to be told, that you have a heart as sinful as the common wretches that crawl on the earth. This is highly offensive and insulting; and I cannot but wonder that your lady-ship should relish any sentiments so much at variance with high rank and good breeding.[6]

Paul's pronouncement that we are "alienated from God . . . enemies . . . [with] evil behavior" may sound a bit harsh to us too, but it is terribly true. All it takes is a telling difficulty, like floating on the cold Atlantic, to find out what is really there.

Humanity's condition is terrible, but God's reconciling purpose is "to present you holy in his sight, without blemish and free from accusation" (v. 22). While the Scriptures paint the darkest possibilities for man apart from Christ, they also give us the highest, noblest vision of man known to any religious conception anywhere! When one is reconciled to Christ, he or she will be presented before him as holy, without blame, and beyond reproach. This person is a "co-heir" of Christ's promises (Romans 8:17) and will remain eternally glorious and holy. If we have been reconciled, this is our position before God right now, and it will be increasingly true in our life as we grow into his image. R. C. Sproul tells us:

> Luther used a simple analogy to explain it. He described the condition of a patient who was mortally ill. The doctor proclaimed that he had medicine that would surely cure the man. The instant the medicine was administered, the doctor declared that the patient was well. At that instant the patient was still sick, but as soon as the medicine passed his lips and entered his body the patient began to get well. So it is with our reconciliation and justification. As soon as we truly believe, that very instant we start to get better; the process of becoming pure and holy is underway and its future completion is certain.[7]

Fellow-believers, in light of our reconciliation we ought to do everything in our power to be practically blameless and holy in this life.

We must become what we are in the Lord. We must submit ourselves ever more completely to the "God who works in you" (Philippians 2:13). Practical holiness should be our life's business.

THE FATHER'S RECONCILING CONDITION (v. 23)

> ... if you continue in your faith, established and firm, not moved from the hope held out in the gospel. This is the gospel that you heard and that has been proclaimed to every creature under heaven, and of which I, Paul, have become a servant.

Paul is not expressing doubt as to whether they will continue on; that is not what the Greek construction means. The scholar Peter O'Brien paraphrases the idea: "At any rate if you stand firm in the faith — and I am sure you will."[8] The positive application of Paul's words are this: the gospel does not work like magic. The mind, the heart, and the will must be involved. Our minds must feed on Christ and his Word. Our hearts are to focus on him in love. Our wills are to take their practice and pattern from him. Present faith leads to present results; present drinking is for present thirst. We must fill our lives every day from him.

It is imperative that all of us be reconciled to Christ. Without reconciliation we will remain adrift on the cold seas — alienated from God, from creation, and from others, though we may wish otherwise. God wants to reconcile us. He enjoys reconciling. His Son endured the Cross "for the joy set before him" (Hebrews 12:2). What God has in mind for us is the greatest vision ever conceived for any mortal. There is only one thing to do, and that is to say yes.

D. L. Moody related this incident between his sister and her son:

> My sister, I remember, told me her boy said something naughty one morning, when his father said to him, "Sammy, go and ask your mother's forgiveness." "I won't," replied the child. "If you don't ask your mother's forgiveness I'll put you to bed." It was early in the morning — before he went to business and the boy didn't think he would do it. He said "I won't" again. They undressed him and put him to bed. The father came home at noon expecting to find his boy playing about the house. He didn't see him about, and asked his wife where he was. "In bed still." So he went up to the room, and sat down by the bed, and said: "Sammy, I want you to ask your mother's forgiveness." But the answer was "No." The father coaxed and begged, but could not induce the

child to ask forgiveness. The father went away, expecting certainly that when he came home at night the child would have got all over it. At night, however, when he got home he found the little fellow still in bed. He had lain there all day. He went to him and tried to get him to go to his mother, but it was no use. His mother went and was equally unsuccessful. That father and mother could not sleep any that night. They expected every moment to hear the knock at their door by their little son. How they wanted to forgive the boy. My sister told me it was just as if death had come into their home. She never passed through such a night. In the morning she went in to him and said: "Now, Sammy, you are going to ask my forgiveness." But the boy turned his face to the wall and wouldn't speak. The father came home at noon and the boy was as stubborn as ever. It looked as though the child was going to conquer. It was for the good of the boy that they didn't want to give him his own way. It is a great deal better for us to submit to God than have our own way. Our own way will lead us to ruin; God's way leads to life everlasting. The father went off to his office, and that afternoon my sister went in to her son about four o'clock and began to reason with him, and, after talking for some time, she said, "Now, Sammy, say 'mother.'" "Mother," said the boy. "Now say 'for.'" "For." "Now just say 'give.'" And the boy repeated "give." "Me," said the mother. "Me," and the little fellow fairly leaped out of bed. "I have said it," he cried; "take me down to papa, so that I can say it to him."9

What a picture of how we are! Just those words, "Father, forgive me," said from the heart, bring us to God.

5

The Supreme Ministry

COLOSSIANS 1:24-29

R. C. Sproul, president of Ligonier Study Center, a popular theologian and a gifted and colorful communicator, tells of having the following exchange with one of his students:

> I remember a starry-eyed college student who looked at me and said in wonderment, "What was it like for you when you were just a minister?" I lost it. I exploded in a paroxysm of indignation. "What do you mean *just* a minister? Don't you realize that the parish ministry is the highest calling on earth? God had only one Son and He made Him a preacher!"[1]

In my mind's eye I see Dr. Sproul at his theatrical best, standing over his student like a latter-day Luther, while the student is trying to find somewhere to hide. Actually Sproul was just having fun, but he was serious about his point, which is that the Christian ministry is the highest calling.

Of course Sproul is not the first to think this way. John Wycliffe, the English "Morning Star" of the Reformation, wrote:

> The highest service that men may attain to on earth is to preach the Word of God. This service falls peculiarly to priests and therefore God more straightly demands it of them. . . . And for this cause, Jesus Christ left other works and occupied himself mostly in preaching, and thus did his apostles, and for this God loved them.[2]

In the last century, Alexander Whyte of Edinburgh wrote to a discouraged pastor, "The angels around the throne envy you your great work. . . . Go on and grow in grace and power as a gospel preacher."[3] In our own day, W. E. Sangster of the Westminster Central Hall in London said:

> Called to preach! . . . commissioned of God to teach the word! A herald of the great King! A witness of the Eternal Gospel! Could any work be more high and holy! To this supreme task God sent his only begotten Son. In all the frustration and confusion of the times, is it possible to imagine a work comparable in importance with that of proclaiming the will of God to wayward men?[4]

And indeed, notwithstanding the fact that we are called to many different occupations and all of them holy if they are God's will, the gospel ministry in its various forms is the highest call possible.

Having introduced us in succession to the supremacy of Christ in creation (vv. 15-17), in the Church (v. 18), and in reconciliation (vv. 19-23), Paul now gives us a supremely magnificent perspective on his resulting ministry. It is a remarkably balanced view which delineates four aspects of his own ministry: his ministerial *attitude*, his ministerial *charge*, his ministerial *purpose*, and his ministerial *devotion*. It will be especially profitable for those who are in the professional ministry, but it ought to prove equally helpful for every serious believer, because we are all called to the "ministry," whatever our stated vocation.

PAUL'S MINISTERIAL ATTITUDE (v. 24)

> Now I rejoice in what was suffered for you, and I fill up in my flesh what is still lacking in regard to Christ's afflictions, for the sake of his body, which is the church.

Paul explicitly said he rejoiced in his sufferings. From a secularist perspective, what he says is incomprehensible — "baptized masochism." But Romans 5:3 speaks of exulting in tribulation; 1 Peter 4:13 says to suffer and rejoice; Acts 5:41 tells of the apostles rejoicing that they had been counted "worthy" to suffer. Paul too rejoiced. But why?

First, because his suffering brought good to the Church. "Now I rejoice in what was suffered for you, and I fill up in my flesh what is still lacking . . . for the sake of his body, which is the church." Without his willingness to suffer (described in 2 Corinthians 11, where he listed an amazing catalogue of miseries he had undergone to bring the gospel to

Asia), there would have been no church in Asia. The gospel has always spread through missionary hardship. But there is something more here, and it is far more subtle: believers grow through their personal suffering, and the good they receive flows to others — thus edifying the Church.

John Newton, the author of "Amazing Grace," said:

> God appoints his ministers to be sorely exercised, both from without and within; that they may sympathize with their flock, and know in their own hearts the deceitfulness of sin, the infirmities of the flesh, and the way in which the Lord supports and bears all who trust in Him.

God's servants benefit, and everyone benefits. For Paul, this is cause for rejoicing. This is why very often the suffering of a brother or sister in Christ is a great source of blessing to the Church, for their elevated character is transferred to fellow believers.

Secondly, Paul described his suffering as "fill[ing] up in my flesh what is still lacking in regard to Christ's afflictions." This is one of the most debated verses in all of Scripture! Whole books have been written on its interpretation over the last 2,000 years.[5] We know it does *not* mean that Paul made up that which was lacking in the atoning sufferings of Christ, for the whole of Colossians as well as the rest of the New Testament teaches the sufficiency of Christ in atonement (cf. 2:13, 14; 1:12-14, 19-22). Paul did not help with the Atonement; that was Christ's solo work. But one thing that the phrase does teach for sure (and everyone agrees on this) is that a close identification develops between Christ and the Church through suffering. Before Paul's Damascus Road encounter, Paul had been making Christ suffer in the people he was persecuting. Christ's first words to Saul made this clear: "Saul, Saul, why do you persecute me?" (Acts 9:4). Jesus was being persecuted in the bodies of his followers. However, immediately after Paul's conversion Jesus said, "I will show him how much he must suffer for my name" (9:16). Now Paul would suffer, and Christ would suffer in him — a stupendous truth!

Dr. Helen Roseveare, a British medical doctor, has served more than twenty years in Zaire, Africa. For twelve and a half years she had a frenetic but generally wonderful time serving as the only doctor to an area containing more than half a million people (today about one and a half million). But in 1964 revolution overwhelmed the country, and she and her coworkers were thrown into five and a half months of almost unbelievable brutality and torture. On one occasion when Dr. Roseveare was on the verge of being executed, a seventeen-year-old student came to her defense and was savagely beaten as a result. He was kicked about like a football and left for dead. Dr. Roseveare was sick. For a moment she thought that God had forsaken her, even though she did not doubt his reality. But God stepped in, overwhelmed her with the sense of his own presence, and said something like this: "Twenty years ago you asked me for the privilege of being a missionary, the privilege of being identified with me. These are not your sufferings; they are my sufferings." As the force of that hit home, the doctor said she was overcome with a great sense of privilege. Helen Roseveare's sense of identification with Christ, of union with him, was elevated by her suffering, and she rejoiced. Paul likewise rejoiced in the sublime oneness he sensed as Christ participated with him in his sufferings.

How then did Paul fill up "what is still lacking in regard to Christ's afflictions"? No one knows for sure. Many top scholars today, such as Ralph Martin and Peter O'Brien, believe that Paul's words have reference to the common Jewish understanding that the Messianic Age was to be preceded by a definite amount of suffering (1 Enoch 47:14; 2 Baruch 30:2). Thus the sufferings are the sufferings of God's people, but they are ultimately Christ's sufferings because of his identity with his people. So Paul in his sufferings helped fulfill Christ's and thus hastened the Messianic Age.[6] If this is the correct interpretation, Paul was rejoicing because his sufferings (which are Christ's sufferings) were bringing the total nearer the ultimate goal and hastening the day of the Kingdom.

However that may be, one thing is clear: Paul knew his sufferings were good for the Church and that they brought to him a special closeness with Christ. Every blow that fell on him fell on his Master, and thus bound them even closer together in mutual suffering. Paul's experience was like that of Shadrach, Meshach, and Abednego who in the fiery furnace were joined by a fourth person: the Lord (Daniel 3:25). That is why Paul could pray from a Roman jail:

> I want to know Christ and the power of his resurrection and the fellowship of sharing in his sufferings, becoming like him in his death. (Philippians 3:10)

Paul knew sufferings are miserable, but the resulting sense of union with Christ is wonderful.

PAUL'S MINISTERIAL CHARGE (vv. 25-27)

> I have become its [the Church's] servant by the commission God gáve me to present to you the word of God in its fullness. . . . (v. 25)

This charge has preaching as its main function, and specifically Biblical exposition. The phrase "to present to you the word of God" literally reads, "that I might complete the Word of God." The idea is to lay out the Word of God fully. People cannot know Christ better without knowing the Scriptures. Preaching (exposition) was the heart of God's call to Paul.

Preaching must open the Word of God. Paul affirms here such preaching is primary to an authentic ministry. There is no shortcut — it takes work. Joseph Parker put it this way:

> If I had talked all the week, I could not have preached on Sunday. That is all. Mystery there is none. I have made my preaching work my delight, the very festival of my soul. That is all. Young brother, go thou and do likewise, and God bless thee![7]

The specifics of this preaching are given in verses 26 and 27:

> . . . the mystery that has been kept hidden for ages and generations, but is now disclosed to the saints. To them God has chosen to make known among the Gentiles the glorious riches of this mystery, which is Christ in you, the hope of glory.

Paul's preaching set forth a "mystery" — namely, that in some way God's saving purpose was going to be extended to the Gentiles (Isaiah 49:6; Romans 15:9-12). From the ancient Jewish perspective, this seemed impossible because of the mutual disdain which Gentiles and especially Jews had for one another. It was a mystery indeed!

Bishop John Green of Sydney tells about working with a group of boys, some of aboriginal blood and some of English descent, and how the racial tensions were such that they would not sit peaceably with each other on the bus. One day when things were out of hand, he stopped the bus, ordered them all out, and told them they were no longer black and white, but green. He lined them up in alternate order and made each one say, "I'm green," as he got back on the bus. They drove along quietly "integrated," until he heard a voice from the back of the bus say, "OK, light green on one side and dark green on the other!"

The ancient Jews and Gentiles were like that, but with distinctly less humor, and their animosities went far beyond skin. The prophesied reconciliation of Jews and Gentiles was truly a mystery. Then Christ came, and the middle wall was broken down, and Jews and Gentiles became together a new man establishing *shalom*, peace (Ephesians 2:13-18).

... the mystery of Christ, which was not made known to men in other generations as it has now been revealed by the Spirit to God's holy apostles and prophets. This mystery is that through the gospel the Gentiles are heirs together with Israel, members together of one body, and sharers together in the promise in Christ Jesus. (Ephesians 3:4-6)

Jews and Gentiles all sat down at one table and counted themselves one in Christ. It was a miracle! This had come about only because of "Christ in you, the hope of glory" (v. 27b). The indwelling of the Lord Jesus Christ is what made the miracle possible.

This happened in Colosse, and it can happen today. One of the greatest glories of the gospel is that it brings people who are different from each other together.

PAUL'S MINISTERIAL PURPOSE (v. 28)

We proclaim him, admonishing and teaching everyone with all wisdom, so that we may present everyone perfect in Christ.

Paul's goal is nothing short of presenting to Christ complete, mature, full-grown Christians. He was not into the "I'll save 'em, you raise 'em!" type of thinking. Rather, his great joy was to present to Christ believers who have reached their maximum earthly potential.

For what is our hope, our joy, or the crown in which we will glory in the presence of our Lord Jesus when he comes? Is it not you? Indeed, you are our glory and joy. (1 Thessalonians 2:19, 20)

Listen to Paul's benediction in 1 Thessalonians 5:23:

May God himself, the God of peace, sanctify you through and through. May your whole spirit, soul and body be kept blameless at the coming of our Lord Jesus Christ.

Paul's means of bringing believers to maturity, according to verse 28, was threefold: proclamation, admonishment, and teaching.

He *proclaimed* Christ; Christ was the beginning and the end of his message. As George Whitefield said, "Other men may preach the gospel better than I, but no man can preach a better gospel."

When the preaching of Christ brought converts, Paul spent time *"admonishing . . . everyone,"* which means that he corrected and warned them. Paul did not shrink from this unpleasant task of admonishment, because he cared. I understand that when Henrietta Mears, one of the most effective Christians of our time, entered a room, people often had the feeling that she was saying to each person, "Where have you been? I've been looking all over for you."[8] This was certainly the way it was with Paul.

He also spent his time "*teaching* everyone." The Greek text of verse 28 is emphatic, mentioning "everyone" three times.[9] Paul proclaimed Christ and admonished and taught everyone because he truly believed Christ was for everyone, and he saw great potential in every soul he touched. What a way to look at life!

PAUL'S MINISTERIAL ENERGY (v. 29)

> To this end I labor, struggling with all his energy, which so powerfully works in me.

The truth is, no one can hope to have a Biblically authentic ministry without hard work. Paul's language in this verse is brutally compelling. The Greek word translated "labor" was used for work which left one so weary it was as if the person had taken a beating. It denotes labor to exhaustion.[10] "Struggling," a stronger term than "labor," was the Greek word from which we derive the English word *agony* and was used for agonizing in an athletic event or in a fight.[11] The words together describe the tremendous energy of Paul's apostolic ministry. He strained every physical and moral sinew to present every man complete in Christ. First Thessalonians 2:9 pictures this:

> Surely you remember, brothers, our toil and hardship; we worked night and day in order not to be a burden to anyone while we preached the gospel of God.

It is often said, "When all is said and done, there is more said than done." It ought not to be that way! Luther worked so hard that many days, according to his biographers, he fell into bed. Moody's bedtime prayer on one occasion, as he rolled his bulk into bed, was, "Lord, I'm tired! Amen." John Wesley rode sixty to seventy miles many days of his life and preached an average of three sermons a day, whether he was riding or not. Alexander Maclaren would get to his office when the workmen went to work so he could hear their boots outside, and would put on workmen's boots to remind him why he was in his study. G. Campbell Morgan kept a newspaper clipping for twenty years, entitled "Sheer Hard Work," and said:

What is true of the minister is true of every man who bears the name of Christ. We have not begun to touch the great business of salvation when we have sung, "Rescue the perishing, care for the dying." We have not entered into the business of evangelizing the city or the world until we have put our own lives into the business, our own immediate physical endeavor, inspired by spiritual devotion.[12]

Paul's ministerial drive is a model for us all. We will never have an authentic, apostolic ministry unless we are willing to work to the point of exhaustion.

R. C. Sproul is right: the ministry of the gospel is a glorious thing. But we do not have to be an apostle or a reformer or a preacher to do it. Some years ago a woman in Africa became a Christian. Being filled with gratitude, she decided to do something for Christ. She was blind, uneducated, and seventy years of age. She came to her missionary with her French Bible and asked her to underline John 3:16 in red ink. Mystified, the missionary watched her as she took her Bible and sat in front of a boys' school in the afternoon. When school dismissed, she would call a boy or two and ask them if they knew French. When they proudly responded that they did, she would say, "Please read the passage underlined in red." When they did, she would ask, "Do you know what this means?" And she would tell them about Christ. The missionary says that over the years twenty-four young men became pastors due to her work.[13] She had it all:

- a ministerial attitude.
- a ministerial charge.
- a ministerial purpose.
- a ministerial energy.

This call is for all of us!

6

The Supreme Concern

COLOSSIANS 2:1-5

W. E. Sangster was once interviewing applicants for the Methodist ministry when an interesting young man presented himself before the committee. When it came his time to speak, the would-be preacher said he felt that he ought to explain that he was rather shy and not the sort of person who would set the Thames River on fire — that is, stir up the city. Dr. Sangster responded with consummate wisdom:

> My dear young brother, I'm not interested to know if you could set the Thames on fire. What I want to know is this: if I picked you up by the scruff of your neck and dropped you into the Thames, would it sizzle?[1]

Dr. Sangster was looking for something apostolic, something passionate, something Pauline in the young candidate. The Apostle Paul was indeed a passionate man. It is said that when George Whitefield's preaching was getting people out of their beds in Edinburgh, a man on the way to the great tabernacle met David Hume, the Scottish philosopher and skeptic. Surprised at meeting him on his way to hear Whitefield preach, the man said, "I thought you did not believe in the gospel." To which Hume replied, "I don't, but he does."[2] Paul was like Whitefield; or better, Whitefield was like Paul.

In Colossians 2:1-5 Paul states his specific concerns for the Colossian church. Up to this point, this is by far the most personal part of the letter. In expressing his concern, he models for us what and how our hearts ought to feel for the Church.

COLOSSIANS
THE INTENSITY OF PAUL'S CONCERN (v. 1)

> I want you to know how much I am struggling for you and for
> those at Laodicea, and for all who have not met me personally.

In mentioning his struggle, Paul again uses the noun *agon* from
which we get *agony*. The word originally was derived from the place
where the Greeks assembled for their Olympic games, a place where they
agonized in wrestling and footraces, where they fought to win.[3] Paul had
been agonizing, fighting for the Colossians with everything he had.

What makes this truly remarkable is that he had never once personally visited them or their neighboring churches. Aside from Epaphras,
Philemon, and perhaps a few others he had met in Ephesus, he had never
seen the Colossians. He had no idea what the people looked like, he knew
nothing of their personalities; yet he agonized for them. Why this strain
for people he had never seen? Because he was God's "chosen instrument"
to bring the gospel to the Gentiles (Acts 9:15). His old stony heart had
been replaced with an apostolic heart which beat with love for the
despised Gentiles. It was like the heart of the shoemaker William Carey,
some eighteen centuries later, who made a leather globe so he could pray
for a world still unseen to him. Ultimately Carey's "world-class" heart
propelled him to India as he became the founder of modern missions.

But there was even more, for Paul and the Colossians shared the
same relationship with Christ. He was also their spiritual father because
he had won them through Epaphras. All of these elements contributed to
his dynamic, agonizing struggle, and perhaps his persecution as well. (He
was in prison when writing this letter.) Wherever Paul went, there was
conflict: riots in Ephesus, beatings in Philippi, stoning in Lystra, shipwreck at sea, dangers everywhere. Paul bared his heart in 2 Corinthians
1:8.

> We do not want you to be uninformed, brothers, about the hard-
> ships we suffered in the province of Asia. We were under great
> pressure, far beyond our ability to endure, so that we despaired
> even of life.

The words he used here described a beast of burden which had
fallen and could not get up because the load was so heavy. This was how
Paul felt in Asia — he thought he was going to die.

There was also the *agon* of labor. It was a struggle to work night
and day so as not to be a burden to anyone, just to present the gospel
(1 Thessalonians 2:9). In addition, there was the *agon* that came from car-

52

ing so much how his converts were doing that he said, "Who is weak, and I do not feel weak? Who is led into sin, and I do not inwardly burn?" (2 Corinthians 11:29). It hurts to care, and there were nights when Paul tossed and turned as he thought about his converts and empathized with their ups and downs.

But most of all, he wrestled in prayer for them. That is where the real fight was (and is)! In 4:12, he told how faithful Epaphras was "always wrestling in prayer for you" (the same word as in 2:1!). In Ephesians 6, where he described how to put on the full armor of God so as to do battle, he concluded by telling the fully armed warrior to:

> . . . pray in the Spirit on all occasions with all kinds of prayers and requests. With this in mind, be alert and always keep on praying for all the saints. (v. 18)

This is where the greatness of his struggle for the Colossian believers lay! Paul agonized in prayer for people he had never met.

What a great heart was Paul's! Enlarged hearts always know the *agon*. They have sleepless nights; they empathize; they struggle in prayer. But these big hearts also know the most joy. It is this kind of heart to which all of us are called, whether we are missionaries or merchants: a heart that is willing to agonize not only over our own little circle, but the Church Universal.

There is a pastor in Chicago who likes to say: "When the tide is in, all the ships are riding high. When the Holy Spirit is working, then we'll all be riding high; none of us will be scraping bottom." His concern is not just for his church, but for the greater Church. If we have a heart like Paul's, we won't just pray for our little fellowship group or for the church we attend — we'll pray for other churches in our city, we'll pray for the world.

THE HEART OF PAUL'S CONCERN (vv. 2, 3)

> My purpose is that they may be encouraged in heart and united in love, so that they may have the full riches of complete understanding, in order that they may know the mystery of God, namely, Christ, in whom are hidden all the treasures of wisdom and knowledge.

Perceptive Christians have always known that the key to spiritual well-being is an increased knowledge and focus upon Christ. Less than one month before C. S. Lewis died, he wrote this letter to a little girl:

53

Dear Ruth . . . Many thanks for your kind letter, and it was very good of you to write and tell me that you like my books; and what a very good letter you write for your age! If you continue to love Jesus, nothing much can go wrong with you, and I hope you may always do so.[4]

What you think of Christ, your conception of him, is *everything*. If you believe in Jesus Christ, that he is eternal, without beginning and without end, that he always was continuing; if you believe that he is creator of everything, every cosmic speck across trillions of light-years of trackless space, the creator of the textures and shapes and colors which daily dazzle your eyes; if you believe that he is the sustainer of all creation, the force which is presently holding the atoms of your body, your town, this universe together, and that without him all would dissolve; if you believe that he is the mystery, the incarnate reconciler who will one day reconcile the universe and redeem humanity to himself; if you believe that he is the lover of your soul, who loves you with a love bounded only by his infinitude; then, despite the fact that life will be full of trouble, nothing much will go wrong. Your vision of Christ will quicken and shape your life. What you believe about Christ makes all the difference in the world now and in eternity.

How does this knowledge of Christ come? Through brotherly love in the Church.

> . . . that they may be encouraged in heart and united in love, so that
> they may have the full riches of complete understanding. (v. 2)

In other words, depth of understanding is facilitated when believers' hearts are bound together in love.

F. F. Bruce comments: "Paul emphasizes that the revelation of God cannot be properly known apart from the cultivation of brotherly love within the Christian community."[5]

This means that mere intellectual comprehension of the mystery of Christ will not bring full understanding of the mystery, for understanding also comes through the love of Christians one for another. How is this so? When we are loved by other believers, we experience Christ through them, and thus our knowledge of Christ is enhanced. The complementary side of this is that when we allow the Holy Spirit through us to live the life of Christ (and we experience this when we do acts of love toward members of the Body of Christ), then too we have our knowledge of him enhanced. If we love, there are "full riches of complete understanding."

This is an important message for an alive Christianity. No intellectual process will lead to a full grasp of the mystery of Christ unless it is accompanied by a love for him and for Christians that knits us, the Church, together in love. We cannot pursue knowledge of God in willful, unloving isolation, rejecting fellowship with others. Historically, some have tried and have suffered incomplete or even distorted understanding. "Complete" understanding of the mystery comes in loving community.

This was so for both Luther and Calvin. Their lives were filled with people, for they were great lovers of the Body of Christ. The same was true of the great John Wesley. The deepest knowledge of the mystery of Christ comes from both the head and the heart. We must study the Scriptures about him intensely, with all our heart, and we must love him and his people with all our heart — and then we will know as we ought.

So when brotherly love is present and continuing, it facilitates a profound knowledge of Christ, which in turn results in wisdom and knowledge. This connection was underscored by Paul at the end of verse 2 and in verse 3 where he states his desire:

> . . . that they may know the mystery of God, namely, Christ, in whom are hidden all the treasures of wisdom and knowledge.

This was a swing at the Gnostic heretics who claimed to have the way to wisdom and knowledge. Paul said there was (and is) no other treasury of knowledge, for "all the treasures of wisdom and knowledge" are in Christ. Of this truth Alexander Maclaren remarked:

> In Christ, as in a great storehouse, lie all the riches of spiritual wisdom, the massive ingots of solid gold which when coined into creeds and doctrines are the wealth of the Church. All which we can know concerning God and man, concerning sin and righteousness and duty, concerning another life, is in Him Who is the home and deep mine where truth is stored. . . . The central fact of the universe and the perfect encyclopaedia of all moral and spiritual truth is Christ, the Incarnate Word, the Lamb slain, the ascended King.[6]

Here's the point: when we love him and love the Scriptures and love the Church so that we are united in love with each other, the mystery unfolds and we are in touch with "all the treasures of wisdom and knowledge." It can be so now, if we know Christ. It ought to be so. The fact is, this treasure is meant to grow in this life and in eternity. There is really nothing beyond the truth that "God so loved the world that he gave his one and only Son" (John 3:16). Grasped even imperfectly, this brings life.

But as it is loved and lived, it brings undreamed light and warmth with each million miles until it fills the entire sky. As Christians we grow toward Christ and he fills more and more of our horizon until there is no sky — only him and his riches.

The heart of Paul's concern was that the Colossians would grow ever more toward Christ. He was concerned for their minds, and that is why the bulk of the first chapter presents such a heady picture of Christ. But he was also concerned for their hearts, because the journey involved a heart's love for Christ and fellow-believers. Can you say:

I love Thy Kingdom, Lord,
The House of Thine abode,
The Church our blest Redeemer saved
With His own precious blood.

For her my tears shall fall;
For her my prayers ascend,
For her my cares and toils be giv'n,
Till toils and cares shall end.[7]

If you can say these words to God, you are on your way to a deeper knowledge of Christ.

THE MOTIVATION BEHIND PAUL'S CONCERN (vv. 4, 5)

Paul was motivated to say all of the above because he was concerned that the Colossians were being led astray. In verse 4 we read, "I tell you this so that no one may deceive you by fine-sounding arguments." The Gnostics' clever arguments could easily lead astray those who were not knit together in brotherly love and thus fully enjoying the treasures of Christ's wisdom and knowledge. It was an important warning in Paul's day, and it is equally *apropos* today when the means of persuasion are so highly developed. We are subject to space-age subtleties which the apostle could never have imagined. For our souls' sake, there must be a deep, growing knowledge of Christ and a love among us!

That was part of Paul's motivation. The other part, the positive part, is seen in verse 5, and here we come full circle:

For though I am absent from you in body, I am present with you in spirit and delight to see how orderly you are and how firm your faith in Christ is.

The Spirit of God had united both Paul and the Colossians to Christ. Because they all lived in Christ, Paul was present in spirit with them, "struggling" on their behalf. Paul 's great heart sizzled!

Paul's passion was that the Church might be "united in love" so that it would attain the mystery of God—namely, Christ. This ought to be our passion.

> *Thou, O Christ, art all I want;*
> *More than all in Thee I find.*

Let us journey toward the Son until he fills the whole sky.

7

The Supreme Charge

COLOSSIANS 2:6, 7

Twenty-five years ago I was beginning the final stretch of my freshman year in college on the West Coast. I was pleased and impressed with everything, but nothing impressed me more than one of my friends in Greek class. He was a senior and the "complete" collegian: student body president; captain and star halfback on the football team; big, handsome, with a ready smile; and quite intelligent. His family seemed to know all the Christian leaders in the world. To top it off, he was a nice person. I was impressed — really impressed!

Due to circumstances, it was necessary for me to continue my education elsewhere after my freshman year, and I lost track of my acquaintance until a few years later when a mutual acquaintance handed me a copy of the student newspaper of a major California university, featuring a front-page photograph of a professor posing nude in his classroom with some of his students, males and females alike. The professor was my old acquaintance. Subsequent articles in the *Los Angeles Times* revealed that he was the leader of a group of campus radicals and that he now expounded a crude nihilism which had led him to write a book intentionally using bad grammar and filthy language. The university, noted for its tolerance of viewpoint, was trying to kick him out (and later succeeded). How I sorrowed at the news!

Apostasy can come to those who appear to be the best of Christians. I have even seen colleagues in the ministry fall to the lure of what they considered "deeper things." I remember one in particular who would no longer discuss the meaning of Scripture with me or others because he had a "higher hermeneutic," by which he meant that because he meditated on Scripture so much, he could see truths that transcended grammatical and traditional theological interpretation. With self-proclaimed "superior knowledge," he fathered a terrible legalism and led many into a false cult.

Paul was aware that the Gnostics were offering "deeper knowledge" to the Colossians. He knew well their tactics: coming as wiser, more mature brethren who claimed that "love" had compelled them to help lift the Colossian Christians from their baby-faith up to the real thing. In verses 6 and following he went on the offense against these false teachers.

So then, just as you received Christ Jesus as Lord, continue to live in him, rooted and built up in him, strengthened in the faith as you were taught, and overflowing with thankfulness. (vv. 6, 7)

Here we have Paul's protective charge to the Colossians. What is the walk that protects us like?

A BIRTH WALK (v. 6)

"So then, just as you received Christ Jesus as Lord, continue to live in him." This means our experience of first coming to Christ ought to mirror how we walk in him all the days of our lives. What was our spiritual genesis like?

When we were born again, we "received Christ Jesus as Lord." Receiving him means more than simply accepting him. The Colossians received the teaching and tradition handed down about Christ. They did not receive him just as Jesus or just as Christ, but in his fullness. They received him as the "Christ," the Anointed One or the Messiah. They received him as the One who fulfilled all the Messianic prophesies of the Old Testament. He was their Divine Prophet, Priest, and King.

They also received him as "Jesus," a historical person rooted in humanity through the Incarnation. *Jesus* is Greek for the Hebrew name *Joshua*, which means, "the Lord is salvation." So they received him as the captain of salvation, and so rejected salvation in any other name (Acts 4:12).

And they received him as "Lord." "Lord" gathers up all that Paul had previously said about Christ in Colossians.[1] It is a dynamic, comprehensive title. When the Colossians received him, they received him in full knowledge of this teaching, and they bowed before him as their Sovereign, their Lord!

Billy Graham says in *The Annals of America*:

No man can be said to be truly converted to Christ who has not bent his will to Christ. He may give intellectual assent to the claims of Christ and may have had emotional religious experiences; however, he is not truly converted until he has surrendered his will to Christ as Lord, Savior and Master.[2]

Spurgeon comments on this, saying:

It is interesting to notice that the Apostles preached the Lordship of Christ. The word *Savior* occurs only twice in the Acts of the Apostles (Acts 5:31, 13:23). On the other hand it is amazing to notice the title "Lord" is mentioned 92 times; "Lord Jesus" 13 times; and "The Lord Jesus Christ" 6 times in the same book. The Gospel is: "Believe on the Lord Jesus Christ, and thou shalt be saved."[3]

Paul's point is that the Colossians had "received Christ Jesus as Lord" and that they would remain safe from spiritual seduction (apostasy) if they continued to walk in submission to him.

We too will be resistant to the gnosticizing influences around us if we walk in the reality of "Christ Jesus as Lord." The reason the major cults are cults is because they have defective doctrines of Christ. The Mormons, Jehovah's Witnesses, Christian Science, etc., say, like the Gnostics, that they believe in Christ — *but what kind of Christ?* Certainly not the Christ of the Scriptures. This is also true of virulent forms of legalism and some of the extreme forms of the "prosperity gospel" which eat away at the fringes of evangelicalism. The safeguard against this is a perpetual bowing before Christ Jesus, the *Lord*, in line with our initial awareness that we are Christ's and our sins are forgiven.

Recall how it was then? Remember the submission? Remember the joy? Recently I read the conversion account of Charles Simeon of Cambridge, the founder of the evangelical movement in the Church of England. He came to Christ on an Easter morning after a great inner struggle. He said:

I awoke early with those words upon my heart and lips, "Jesus Christ is risen today! Hallelujah! Hallelujah!" From that hour peace flowed in rich abundance into my soul, and at the Lord's Table in our Chapel I had the sweetest access to God through my blessed Saviour.[4]

Remember the humility? Remember the gratitude? We are to walk in the new-birth realities. Paul makes this a present, active imperative: "continue to live." There must be ongoing progress in this genesis way.

A WALK IN HIM (vv. 6b, 7a)

". . . continue to live in him, rooted and built up in him." When I was in grade school, our family home sat across the street from twenty-five acres. Each year thousands of huge tumbleweeds would grow, turn brown, and await the first strong wind. When that happened, there were tumbleweeds all over the place, which we gathered and burned. Tumbleweeds have a single, rather narrow root which turns brittle with age. Their limited root structure results in a short life, death, and subjection to the will of the winds.

The Colossian Christians, in contrast, were "rooted" in Christ. Paul probably had the imagery of Psalm 1 in mind, picturing them as trees that send their roots wide and deep into the soil of Christ, thus drawing from his very life. Believers are in Christ as trees are rooted in the earth. There is absolute dependence on the believer's part. In other passages we read of the vine metaphor (for example, John 15:1-4), and there the image is similar: the life of the vine flows into the branches. With trees, a general rule is that the visible spread of the branches is roughly equal to the invisible spread of the roots. The deeper and more widespread our roots in Christ, the greater shade, fruit, and beauty we provide.

The next metaphor is that of a building: "built up in him." As believers, our foundation rests on Christ and in Christ, and we are to be about the business of enhancing this relationship. We are to dig deep into the soil of Christ, there plant our lives, and spend our remaining days becoming a building worthy of the foundation. Such a life in and upon Christ will not succumb to the sweet gnosticizing of the false teachers. Center down on Christ.

A WALK IN FAITH (v. 7b)

". . . strengthened in the faith as you were taught." They were to continue to be established in the faith which they believed and were taught in the beginning. Growth does not discard the early truths of Jesus Christ for newer truth, as the Gnostics were teaching. Jesus is not a beginning, to be left behind by the "mature." R. C. Lucas, Rector of St. Helen's Church in London, has said:

> This has something uncomfortably trenchant to say to Christian leaders. Did not many owe their first knowledge of Christ to evangelical truth? Yet how many now say that they have "grown out" of such simplicities. But to grow beyond the saving truths as we were faithfully taught them is not to grow up in a way that can

please God or profit the church. Such fancied superiority in knowledge calls for honest self-examination to see if true loyalty to Christ remains.[5]

To outgrow the basic truth of Christianity is to become post-Christian and pagan, despite objections to the contrary. Moreover, the vast doctrines of God (the Incarnation, reconciliation, adoption) would defy exhaustive exposition if we studied them for a thousand years.

Seeing the greatness of the essentials, we need to pray, like the saintly Rutherford, for hearts and minds that are bigger, that we might hold more of Christ. I think Paul's prayer for the Ephesian church applies well here:

> I pray that you, being rooted and established in love, may have power, together with all the saints, to grasp how wide and long and high and deep is the love of Christ, and to know this love that surpasses knowledge — that you may be filled to the measure of all the fullness of God. (Ephesians 3:17-19)

As we love him, we learn more; as we learn more, we love him more. We are not arguing for some sort of cliché-ridden Christianity, but for a profound head-and-heart study of God's Word, with an eye on the magnificent essentials.

A WALK IN THANKFULNESS (v. 7c)

". . . and overflowing with thankfulness." A healthy Christian walk spills over with gratitude and praise. We are not talking about the mindless mouthing of clichés. Two men were walking through a field when suddenly an angry bull chased them. They headed for the fence as fast as they could move. "Say a prayer," cried the one to the other. "I don't know any," answered his huffing and puffing companion. "You've got to," said the first, "that bull is getting closer." "O.K.," shouted his friend, "I'll pray the only one I know." As the horns of the bull came within striking range, the running man offered, "For what we are about to receive, the Lord make us truly grateful!" Paul is not talking about mindless piety, but praise deep in the soul.

Thankfulness is a good test of our spiritual state. A thankless spirit betrays a life which is no longer focusing on the greatness of Christ. It is looking down, not up. Thankful hearts herald spiritual health. Alexander Maclaren wrote insightfully:

63

The life which is all influenced by thanksgiving will be pure, strong, happy, in its continual counting of its gifts, and in its thought of the Giver, and not least happy and beautiful in its glad surrender of itself to Him who has given Himself for and to it. The noblest offering that we can bring, the only recompense which Christ asks, is that our hearts and our lives should say, We thank thee, O Lord. "By Him, therefore, let us offer the sacrifice of praise to God continually." And the continual thanksgiving will ensure continuous growth in our Christian character, and a constant increase in the strength and depth of our faith.[6]

The Gnostics had little success around thankful people, and it is the same today. In fact, the thankful often draw others away from false teaching and to Christ.

It is our duty to give thanks:

... give thanks in all circumstances, for this is God's will for you in Christ Jesus. (1 Thessalonians 5:18)

... always giving thanks to God the Father for everything, in the name of our Lord Jesus Christ. (Ephesians 5:20)

Through Jesus, therefore, let us continually offer to God a sacrifice of praise — the fruit of lips that confess his name. (Hebrews 13:15)

Let the peace of Christ rule in your hearts, since as members of one body you were called to peace. And be thankful. Let the word of Christ dwell in you richly as you teach and admonish one another with all wisdom, and as you sing psalms, hymns and spiritual songs with gratitude in your hearts to God. (Colossians 3:15, 16)

There are enticing voices all around, and, as with the Gnostics, what they say sounds logical. If you are making a counterfeit dollar, you do not use yellow construction paper, cut it in the shape of a triangle, and put Batman's picture in the middle with a big "3" on the corners. Deception looks authentic. It is supported by intelligence, credentials, popularity, even a touch of class. Elsewhere Paul said:

For such men are false apostles, deceitful workmen, masquerading as apostles of Christ. And no wonder, for Satan himself masquerades as an angel of light. It is not surprising, then, if his servants masquerade as servants of righteousness. Their end will be what their actions deserve. (2 Corinthians 11:13-15)

The Devil knows what he is doing. As Screwtape said to Wormwood: "Old error in new dress, is ever error nonetheless."

Memorize the verses we have studied. Keep them close to heart. Understand that the dangers are real and deceptive. Walk the walk that insures.

Thou, O Christ, art all I want,
More than all in Thee I find.

8

The Safeguard
Against Seduction

COLOSSIANS 2:8-10

We do not have to live very long to know that it is easy to fool people, and that it is very easy to be fooled ourselves. Dr. Donald Grey Barnhouse, the great preacher and writer, used to illustrate this by telling of a practical joke which he and his teenaged friends played on some unsuspecting passersby in a large city. His group stood on a busy street corner and stared intently into the air. One of them pointed, while another said (loudly enough to be overheard), "It is not." A third friend argued, "It is so!" At this, one or two people stopped and began to look up in the same direction as Barnhouse and his friends. As the argument grew more heated, others stopped to gaze fixedly at the point his group discussed. Then, one by one, Barnhouse and his friends quietly slipped out of the crowd and gathered a few yards away to watch the results. By this time, some fifteen people were looking into the air. The crowd changed as new passersby came along and joined the group and those who had been staring longest left. Twenty minutes later several people were still looking upward. Several others had gone off to the side and were leaning against a building, looking up for something that was not there and never had been. About his childhood trick, Barnhouse observed:

> That little incident is a good illustration of all the earth-born religions. People talk about having faith; they tell you to look in a direction where there is absolutely nothing. Some people are so

desperately in need of seeing something that they will look till they are almost blind, yet they never catch a glimpse of anything real.[1]

His point is so true. Over my years of ministry, I have seen those who were once perfectly healthy Christians set their sight on and their faith in something which was absolutely nothing! I have seen vibrant Christian young women don floor-length dresses and wear bonnets, all because a "leader" said this was the path to true godliness. I have seen intelligent, college-age men refuse to wear shirts or trousers made of mixed fibers because the Old Testament forbade Israelites to wear clothing that was part wool and part linen (Deuteronomy 22:11). Eventually some of these were led off into a cult.

It is amazingly easy for intelligent people to rest their lives on what will ultimately prove to be nothing. We see them standing on street corners selling their literature. We read of them following their guru to another land, giving him all they have, and dying there. We see them attending religious pep rallies, where they are told that health and wealth are theirs if they will only believe in themselves. We see vast religious empires held together by an enslaving sociology which is almost impossible to escape.

It is possible for seemingly healthy believers to be led astray. It happens every day!

Paul found this to be eminently true of the Colossian church and issued a warning which described the danger and then prescribed the safeguard against spiritual seduction. His charge is delivered in verse 8.

CHARGED TO RESIST (v. 8)

See to it that no one takes you captive through hollow and deceptive philosophy, which depends on human tradition and the basic principles of this world rather than on Christ.

We must first understand that Paul was not putting down philosophy. *Philosophy* simply means "love of wisdom." Everything that had to do with theories about God, the world, and the meaning of human life was called philosophy, both in the pagan and Jewish schools of the day.[2] Both Judaism and Christianity are philosophical because they make holistic claims about the nature of reality and set values to guide life.

What Paul was warning against was a dangerous philosophy made up of both elements of Judaism and Greek Gnosticism. Greek Gnosticism taught that a person must work his or her way up a long series of lesser gods, called emanations, before reaching the ultimate god. Here, false Jewish teachers combined Hebrew rites and ascetic regulations with their philosophy, as a better way to move up the spiritual ladder. It was all very mysterious, complicated, astrological, and snooty. But worst of all, it was very deadly because it mixed some of the truth of Hebrew religion with the delectably enticing mysteries of Eastern mysticism and Greek philosophy. This was presented as "something more" which would elevate the ignorant Colossian Christians from their crude baby-faith to the truly deep things of God. Evidently some succumbed.

Paul's warning here noted four characteristics of this dangerously seductive philosophy.

First, it was "deceptive." It sounded great, but it was empty deceit. We have all heard such talk in politics, academics, religion, and science. It sounds so learned, but it says nothing and sometimes is even inane. Edwin Newman, in his classic *Strictly Speaking*, subtitled "Will America Be the Death of English?" cites an unintentionally humorous example of this, found in a "working paper" of Hampshire College, South Amherst, Massachusetts. Newman says the language of this paper, outlining the plans for the college, has never been equaled.

> . . . that social structure should optimally be the consonant patterned expression of culture; that higher education is enmeshed in a congeries of social and political change; that the field of the humanities suffers from a surfeit of leeching, its blood drawn out by verbalism, explication of text, Alexandrian scholasticism, and the exquisite preciosities and pretentiousness of contemporary literary criticism; that a formal curriculum of academic substance and sequence should not be expected to contain mirabilia which will bring all the educative ends of the college to pass, and that any formal curriculum should contain a high frangibility factor; that the College hopes that the Hampshire student will have kept within him news of Hampshire's belief that individual man's honorable choice is not between immolation in a self but instead trusts that his studies and experience in the College will confirm for him the choice that only education allows: detachment and skill enough to feel, and concern enough to act, with self and society in productive interplay, separate and together; that an overzealous independence reduces linguistics to a kind of cryptographic taxonomy of linguistic forms and that the conjoining of other disciplines and traditional linguistics becomes most crucial as problems of meaning are faced in natural language; and that the College expects its students to wrestle most with questions of the human condition, which are, What does it mean to be human? How can men become more human? What are human beings for?[3]

The Gnostics could talk like that (in their religious realm) and impress and intimidate those who knew no better. Yet, if Gnosticism's basic idea was accepted, then everything became supremely rational, even the most absurd rites and mumbo-jumbo. It is the same way with the modern cults. One of the great, flourishing cults of our day has as its credo this theological couplet:

As God was, man is.
As God is, man can become.

This cult's belief is that God was once a man, but because he lived a virtuous life, he was reincarnated to successively higher lives, until finally he became a god of his own planet, and then the god of Heaven. Today thousands are setting out to become gods!

A classic example is Gordon Hall, the Nautilus sports equipment tycoon, of whom *The Arizona Republic* reports:

He is worth more than $100 million, he says, because it was his goal to be worth more than $100 million before the age of 33. (Others say it is closer to $60 million.) There are other goals. By the time he is 38, he will be a billionaire. By the time his earthly body expires — and he is convinced he can live to be 120 years old — he will assume what he believes to be his just heavenly reward: Gordon Hall will be a god. "We have always existed as intelligences, as spirits," he says. "We are down here to gain a body. As man is now God once was. And as God is now, man can become. If you believe it, then your genetic makeup is to be a god. And I believe it. That is why I believe I can do anything. My genetic makeup is to be a god. My God in heaven creates worlds and universes. I believe I can do anything, too."[4]

Gordon Hall is a highly intelligent man, yet deceived.

The brand of Gnosticism that Paul attacked was perversely rational, yet moral. F. F. Bruce says of the Gnostic philosophies:

The spiritual confidence-tricksters against whom they are put on their guard did not inculcate a godless or immoral way of life; the error of such teaching would have been immediately obvious. Their teaching was rather a blend of the highest elements of natural religion known to Judaism and paganism.[5]

Those trying to lead the Colossians astray were not "bad people" in respect to conventional morals. They may even have exceeded many of the Christians in their lifestyle. Moreover, they were sincere. Their sophisticated language, their stringent rationality within the system, and their self-conscious morality made a huge, religious Venus Fly Trap. These are the hallmarks of the great cults today: seductive, deadly deceit, and as vacuous as a hot air balloon. One day Gordon Hall, like the Gnostics of old, will awake to the reality that he was deceived.

Second, the Gnostic philosophy was purported to come from ancient and primal "human tradition." What this means is that the false teachers presented their philosophy as having "antiquity, dignity and revelational character."[6] Every cult today, even those which claim new revelation, hawk their deceptions as ancient in origin, but now brought to light by historical exigencies, or their own holiness, or the position of the stars, or . . .

Third, this false teaching was demon-controlled, depending on "the basic principles of this world rather than on Christ" (v. 8b). The overwhelming majority of recent commentators tells us that "basic principles" should be translated "elemental spirits," as the RSV and NEB have it.[7] These demonic spirits were thought to control the planetary spheres and thus men's lives — the world order.[8] Paul here argued that these evil forces were in control of this false doctrine and desired to bring the Colossians back into the bondage they knew before Christ.

Certainly this is true of the non-Christian cults in our present day. Read the history of their founders and you will regularly see evidences of supernatural, occult intervention and direction. These "elemental spirits" are just as active today, and their hallmark is that they are not based "on Christ." They may use the name of "Christ," even worship a "Christ." However, they do not mean the Christ who is taught in Scripture, but a Christ of their imaginations, a Christ of the "elemental spirits." Again, the result is bondage.

Last, this false Gnostic philosophy is enslaving. Paul warned, "See to it that no one takes you captive through hollow and deceptive philosophy." The phrase, "take you captive" means to carry off, as prisoners were led away by victorious armies. Cultic teaching asserts a death-like grip on its followers, and few come out of it. Paul is saying, stay away from false teaching if you value your life. "See to it that no one takes you captive." How is it possible for one not to be sucked in by a philosophy which is subtly deceitful in its language, logically compelling within its system of reason, and enticingly moral? The only answer is the fullness of Christ.

REASONS TO RESIST (vv. 9, 10)

"For in Christ all the fullness of the Deity lives in bodily form." He is more than merely God-like. He is more than simply overflowing with the character of God. Rather:

The *essence* of God, undivided and in its whole fullness, dwells in Christ in His exalted state, so that He is the essential and adequate image of God.[9]

This statement that "in Christ all the fullness of the Deity lives in bodily form" forever blasts the Gnostics' idea that the fullness came through the emanations and angelic mediators. We can see the fullness of God in his work in the heavens and creation around us. But in Christ we see the face of God. Christ is the sole Temple of Deity in whom the divine glories are stored. How can we go anywhere else but to him?

This truth is great in itself. It ought to steel us against being taken captive by deceitful, empty philosophies. But there is something else which is utterly breathtaking: Christ, full of Deity, fills us. "[A]nd you have been given fullness in Christ" (v. 10). Christ can hold all the fullness of Deity; we cannot. But we are full of his fullness.

My wife and I once stood on the shore of the vast Pacific Ocean — two finite dots alongside a seemingly infinite expanse. As we stood there, we reflected that if I were to take a pint jar and allow the ocean to rush into it, in an instant my jar would be filled with the fullness of the Pacific. But I could never put the fullness of the Pacific Ocean into my jar! Thinking of Christ, we realize that because he is infinite, he can hold all the fullness of Deity. And whenever one of us finite creatures dips the tiny vessel of our life into him, we instantly become full of his fullness.

From the perspective of our humanity, the capacity of our containers is of greatest importance. Our souls are elastic, so to speak, and there are no limits to possible capacity. We can always open to hold more and more of his fullness. The walls can always stretch further; the roof can always rise higher; the floor can always hold more. The more we receive of his fullness, the more we can receive.

We must also understand that his fullness meets our individual needs. He gives us what the moment requires: wisdom, strength, courage. We must remember, too, that as we continue in him, we experience the satisfaction of his fullness, a continual stream filling and overflowing our lives.

> *He is a path, if any be misled;*
> *He is a robe, if any naked be;*
> *If any chance to hunger, he is bread;*
> *If any be a bondman, he is free;*
> *If any be but weak, how strong is he!*
> *To dead men, life he is, to sick men health,*
> *To blind men sight, and to the needy, wealth.*[10]

If you are full of Christ, and growing in that fullness, if you are overflowing with Christ, the Gnostic appeals of the empty philosophies of our age will bear little appeal to you. If you are full of him, how can you want anything else?

Alexander Maclaren put it this way:

Though all the earth were covered with helpers and lovers of my soul, "as the sand by the sea shore innumerable," and all the heavens were sown with faces of angels who cared for me and succoured me, thick as the stars in the milky way — all could not do for me what I need. Yea, though all these were gathered into one mighty and loving creature, even he were no sufficient stay for one soul of man. We want more than creature help. We need the whole fulness of the Godhead to draw from. It is all there in Christ, for each of us. Whosoever will, let him draw freely. Why should we leave the fountain of living waters to hew out for ourselves, with infinite pains, broken cisterns that can hold no water? All we need is in Christ. Let us lift our eyes from the low earth and all creatures, and behold "no man any more," as Lord and Helper, "save Jesus only," "that we may be filled with all the fullness of God."[11]

Let us covenant with God to invite more of his fullness.

9

The Fullness in Christ

COLOSSIANS 2:11-15

As we take up Paul's words in verses 11 to 15, we find him further elaborating upon how the Colossians' fullness, and by implication our fullness, was accomplished in Christ. He began by explaining that the Colossians were full because being "in him [Christ]," they participated in the events of the Cross—namely, Christ's death, burial, and resurrection. This was foundational to their fullness—and ours.

"IN CHRIST": HIS DEATH, BURIAL, AND RESURRECTION (vv. 11, 12)

Paul describes their participation in Christ's death in verse 11:

> In him you were also circumcised, in the putting off of the sinful nature, not with a circumcision done by the hands of men but with the circumcision done by Christ.

Death. Normally, circumcision does not refer to death, but rather to the common rite of circumcising males on the eighth day by cutting away a small portion of flesh. But here it provides a gruesome metaphor for the Crucifixion.[1] His circumcision on the Cross involved not the stripping away of a small piece of flesh, but the violent removal of his entire body in death. The Colossians, now "in him" as believers, *spiritually* shared in this circumcision, this death. Their "sinful nature" was cut away; they died to their former way of life.

Burial. Paul's emphasis here was that the Colossians really did spiritually participate in Christ's death. He reinforced his point by alluding to their baptism — i.e., their burial with Christ: "having been buried with him in baptism" (v.12a). Peter O'Brien says:

> As the burial of Christ (1 Corinthians 15:4) set the seal upon his death, so the Colossians' burial with him in baptism shows that they were truly involved in his death and laid in his grave. It is not as though they simply died *like* Jesus died, or were buried *as* he was laid in the tomb. . . . The burial proves that a real death has occurred and the old life is now a thing of the past.[2]

The practical implications are immense. When Christ's body was circumcised from him in his death on the Cross, we were circumcised, we died.[3] Paul said in Galatians 2:20 that he was "crucified with Christ." Since we died with him, we do not have to serve sin. Romans 6:6, 7 gives the rationale:

> . . . our old self was crucified with him so that the body of sin might be rendered powerless, that we should no longer be slaves to sin — because anyone who has died has been freed from sin.

The "old self," the person we were before conversion, was crucified with Christ. The "body of sin," formerly a vehicle for sin, has been rendered inoperative. Here is the fullness which Christ has given us. We are free to live life to its fullest — free from the domination of sin. In a world that is always seeking the full life, believers are the only ones for whom it is truly possible.

Resurrection. But there is even more. This fullness reaches full blossom by virtue of the believer's participation in Christ's resurrection:

> . . . in which [or, in him][4] you were also raised up with Him through faith in the working of God, who raised Him from the dead. (v. 12, NASB)

This resurrection is not future, but *now.* When we became part of the Body of Christ by the baptizing and identifying work of the Holy Spirit, we were baptized into the ascension of our Lord Jesus Christ. Thus we have resurrection life now. In fact, we are even seated with Christ in the heavenly places (Ephesians 2:6). As Phillips Brooks said:

> The great Easter truth is not that we are to live newly after death — that is not the great thing — but that we are to be new

here — not so much that we are to live forever, as that we are to, and may, live nobly now.

We are resurrected now! We need to allow this truth to saturate our beings, so it will empower us to live honorably today.

Now if we died with Christ, we believe that we will also live with him. For we know that since Christ was raised from the dead, he cannot die again; death no longer has mastery over him. The death he died, he died to sin once for all; but the life he lives, he lives to God. In the same way, *count yourselves dead to sin but alive to God in Christ Jesus.* (Romans 6:8-11, emphasis mine)

The word "count" means "to set to our account, to compute." We are to reflect on our position in Christ and then to set two things to our account: we are "dead to sin," and we are "alive to God in Christ Jesus." The Colossians possessed a fullness which was created and maintained by the fact that they actually participated in the death, burial, and resurrection of Christ. The practical application for us is this: we are to daily reckon to our account that we died with Christ, that we were buried with him, and that we were resurrected with him. This ought to come into our minds again and again, so that it dominates our being.

"IN CHRIST": DELIVERED FROM BONDAGE (vv. 13-15)

When you were dead in your sins and in the uncircumcision of your sinful nature, God made you alive with Christ. (v. 13) .

"Dead" is the description of the spiritual state of every human being who is apart from Christ. It is not a flattering term, but we cannot escape it.

. . . you were dead in your transgressions and sins, in which you used to live when you followed the ways of this world. . . . (Ephesians 2:1)

Outside of Christ, humanity cannot perceive the truth of divine revelation.

The man without the Spirit does not accept the things that come from the Spirit of God, for they are foolishness to him, and he cannot understand them, because they are spiritually discerned. (1 Corinthians 2:14)

Without Christ, we can do nothing to get life. There must be a sovereign communication of life from God. When Elijah stretched himself upon the dead boy, his heart beat against the stillness of the boy's chest until it kindled life. Even so, Christ must lay his full life on our deadness — and then comes life!

All of us who are believers today were once dead. But through Christ, divine surgery was performed. We were empty, but now we are full. If you have not experienced this, let me assure you that it is *real*. We were dead, blind, empty. Our new relationship requires the most positive of expressions: *life, light, fullness!*

We were not only delivered from the bondage of death, but from the guilt of sin:

> God made you alive with Christ. He forgave us all our sins, having canceled the written code, with its regulations, that was against us and that stood opposed to us; he took it away, nailing it to the cross. (vv. 13b, 14)

The apostle says our guilt was like a "written code" — an IOU signed by our own hand, promising to obey God. This, by our lack of obedience, announced our guilt. The Jews had contracted to obey the Law of Moses (see Deuteronomy 27:14-26; 30:15-20). The Gentiles had countersigned through their consciences to keep the moral Law as they understood it (see Romans 2:14, 15). The burden of guilt was immense. The more they and we sinned, the more the decrees became "against us" and "opposed to us." Christ took the IOUs and nailed them to the Cross above his head (just as the charges were nailed over him by Pilate), and then completely forgave us all. J. B. Phillips's translation catches the idea:

> He has forgiven you all your sins: Christ has utterly wiped out the damning evidence of broken laws and commandments which always hung over our heads, and has completely annulled it by nailing it over his own head on the cross.

Martin Luther experienced the reality of this truth in a dream in which he was visited at night by Satan, who brought to him a record of his own life, written with his own hand. The Tempter said to him, "Is that true, did you write it?" The poor terrified Luther had to confess it was all true. Scroll after scroll was unrolled, and the same confession was wrung from him again and again. At length, the Evil One prepared to take his departure, having brought Luther down to the lowest depths of abject misery. Suddenly the Reformer turned to the Tempter and said: "It is true, every word of it, but write across it all: 'The blood of Jesus Christ, God's Son, cleanses us from all sin.'"

The Colossians were complete, whole, because they had been released from the bondage of guilt. There is no tyranny like that of guilt, and having it lifted is wonderful. It is like escaping the pull of gravity — you feel so light and buoyant. This is why the Colossians were full. This is why they needed nothing else!

Paul concluded his exposition of the fullness that comes from being in Christ by stating that it involves deliverance from the bondage of evil powers. "And having disarmed the powers and authorities, he made a public spectacle of them, triumphing over them by the cross" (v. 15). The "powers and authorities" are the demonic powers arrayed against Christ and his Church. This is a picture of a triumphal procession through the streets in celebration of a military victory, with the conquered rulers and authorities put on display. The image that Paul had in mind can be seen in Plutarch's description of the three-day Triumph given the Roman General Aemilius Paulus upon his return from capturing Macedonia. Great scaffolds were erected in the forum and along the boulevards of Rome for spectator seating, and all of Rome turned out, dressed in festive white. On the first day, 259 chariots displayed in procession the statues, pictures, and colossal images taken from the enemy. On the second day, innumerable wagons bore the armor of the Macedonians. As Plutarch tells it:

> . . . all newly polished and glittering; the pieces of which were piled up and arranged purposely with the greatest art, so as to seem to be tumbled in heaps carelessly and by chance: helmets were thrown upon shields, coats of mail upon graves; Cretan targets, and Thracian bucklers and quivers of arrows, lay huddled amongst horses' bits, and through these there appeared the points of naked swords, intermixed with long Macedonian sarissas. All these arms were fastened together with just so much looseness that they struck against one another as they were drawn along, and made a harsh and alarming noise, so that, even as spoils of a conquered enemy they would not be held without dread.[5]

Following the wagons came 3,000 carrying the enemies' silver in 750 vessels, followed by more treasure. On the third day came the captives, preceded by 120 sacrificial oxen with their horns gilded and their heads adorned with ribbons and garlands, next Macedonian gold, then the captured king's chariot, crown, and armor. Then came the king's servants, weeping, with hands outstretched, begging the crowds for mercy. Next came his children. Then King Perseus himself, clad entirely in black, followed by endless prisoners. Finally came the victorious general,

> ... seated on the chariot magnificently adorned, dressed in a robe of purple, interwoven with gold, and holding a laurel branch in his right hand. All the army, in like manner, with boughs of laurel in their hands, divided into their bands and companies, followed the chariot of their commander; some singing verses, according to the usual custom songs of triumph and the praise of Aemilius's deeds.[6]

In the death, burial, and resurrection of Christ, God the Father achieved a great victory over the evil powers of this world, making "a public spectacle of them." He wants us to see that though they still exist, they are defeated. Satan's demons have been sentenced to be in the train of God's victory parade. Thus, we need no longer fear the outcome of our battle with evil. Christ has conquered! We have conquered! And we *will* conquer!

In view of all this, why look to anyone but Christ for fullness? Cultivate human relationships, but do not look for ultimate fulfillment in them because they will disappoint you. Energetically pursue your career, but do not imagine that you will find transcending fulfillment in it. In Christ we have everything. May our prayer be:

> I want to know Christ and the power of his resurrection and the fellowship of sharing in his sufferings, becoming like him in his death. (Philippians 3:10)

If you are spiritually dead — without resurrection life — under sin — under guilt — empty, Christ invites you to come to him:

> Come, all you who are thirsty, come to the waters; and you who have no money, come, buy and eat! Come, buy wine and milk without money and without cost. Why spend money on what is not bread, and your labor on what does not satisfy? Listen, listen to me, and eat what is good, and your soul will delight in the richest of fare. (Isaiah 55:1, 2)
>
> The Spirit and the bride say, "Come!" And let him who hears say, "Come!" Whoever is thirsty, let him come; and whoever wishes, let him take the free gift of the water of life. (Revelation 22:17)

If you are empty, call out to Christ. Do not let yourself go through another day without coming to him. Be born again, receive life, be filled, be delivered, join the victory parade!

10

The Guarding
of Your Treasure

COLOSSIANS 2:16-23

$\mathbf{S}$everal years ago my wife and I, along with our friends Peter and Anita Deyneka, visited the ancient city of Krakow, Poland. Krakow's magnificent square is bordered on one side by the massive spires of St. Mary's Church. From the great steeple of St. Mary's, a bugle has been sounded every day for the last 700 years. The last note on the bugle is always muted and broken, as if some disaster had befallen the bugler. This 700-year commemoration is in memory of a heroic trumpeter who one night summoned the people to defend their city against the hordes of the invading Tartars. As he was sounding the last blast on his trumpet, an arrow from one of the Tartars struck and killed him. So there is always the muffled note at the end. The Krakovians have never forgotten this heroic warning.

The text under consideration also carries an ancient warning, as the Apostle Paul sounded a note which has brought deliverance to all those through the years who would hear it. Originally a warning for the Colossian church which was being besieged by its cultured enemies, it still pertains today in a world where the Church is beset by equally sophisticated and deadly foes. Here is a powerful bulwark against the very subtle attacks which would rob the believer of his or her fullness.

"DO NOT LET ANYONE JUDGE YOU":
A WARNING AGAINST LEGALISM (vv. 16, 17)

Therefore do not let anyone judge you by what you eat or drink, or with regard to a religious festival, a New Moon celebration or a Sabbath day. These are a shadow of the things that were to come; the reality, however, is found in Christ.

The warning included two areas: diet and days.

Regarding their being judged about diet, there were evidently those who were saying that the way to God and spiritual fullness would be enhanced if the Colossian believers returned to the dietary laws of the Old Testament. As you know, the Old Testament categorized certain foods as clean and unclean (see Leviticus 11:2-20). Unknown to the Jew, there were excellent physical reasons for the Old Testament laws, which Dr. S. I. Macmillen has catalogued in his interesting book, *None of These Diseases*. There were also spiritual reasons, for the distinctions between foods were meant to familiarize God's people with the fact of purity and impurity, and thus to stimulate the conscience in everyday life. But when Jesus came, those dietary laws were abolished.

Jesus said to the Pharisees, who were offended by his liberated eating habits: "'Are you so dull? . . . Don't you see that nothing that enters a man from the outside can make him "unclean"? For it doesn't go into his heart but into his stomach, and then out of his body.' (In saying this, Jesus declared all foods 'clean'" (Mark 7:18-20; cf. Matthew 15:1-20). Peter's vision settled it for him, as he saw a sheet lowered from Heaven, crawling with clean and forbidden animals. Peter was scandalized! "Then a voice told him, 'Get up, Peter. Kill and eat.' 'Surely not, Lord!' Peter replied. 'I have never eaten anything impure or unclean.' The voice spoke to him a second time, 'Do not call anything impure that God has made clean.' This happened three times, and immediately the sheet was taken back to heaven" (Acts 10:13-16).

Paul made this conclusion in 1 Corinthians 8:8 — "But food does not bring us near to God; we are no worse if we do not eat, and no better if we do." So the New Testament Scriptures are unified in telling us that all food and drink are lawful. Of course, dietary principles are a good idea. Eat too many Twinkies and you will no longer be "twinkletoes"; too many Snickers are no laughing matter. But dietary discipline is not a sign of spirituality. We are not to judge others, or allow anyone to pass a religious judgment on us, in regard to food and drink.

The same applies to days. The Jews had their special feast days (Leviticus 25) and their "New Moon" celebrations (Isaiah 1:13) and their Sabbaths (Exodus 20:9-11). When Christ came, he fulfilled them all! We no longer celebrate the Sabbath because we now worship on the "Lord's Day" (Revelation 1:10), the first day of the week (1 Corinthians 16:2; Acts 20:7), the day which commemorates the Resurrection (John 20). Verse 17 says that these things are "a shadow of the things that were to come; the reality, however, is found in Christ." The dietary rules sensitized God's people to purity, the great feasts taught various aspects of Christ's work, and the Sabbath displayed something of the rest into which he leads his people. But they were just "a shadow." The real thing has come in Christ (cf. Luke 24:27).

The idea that spirituality can be quantified provides an unfortunate basis for pride and judgmentalism. The flesh finds doing truly spiritual things difficult, as "the spirit is willing, but the flesh is weak" (Matthew 26:41, NASB). But the flesh has no trouble with religious rules and regulations. There is an authentic lure to legalism.

However, though legalism also has its downside. It spawns *judgmentalism*. Judgmentalism is miserable for the judged and the judging, because it shrivels their souls.

Legalism is intrinsically *joyless*, as the savage tribesman observed when a missionary was trying to convert him. The tribesman was very old and the missionary was very Old Testament, with a version of Christianity which leaned very heavily on the "thou shalt nots." After listening to what the missionary said, the tribesman replied, "To be old and to be Christian, they are the same thing!"[1]

Legalism also demands *uniformity*. Whenever you find legalism dominant, you will find people who dress the same way and use the same speech, posture, and manners — even the same facial expressions! "Do nots" produce a grotesque uniformity.

Lastly, such legalism produces a *surface faith*, because its adherents emphasize the things which are not really important. Their "do nots" ignore deadly sins such as coveting, gossiping, slandering, bitterness, and hatred. Legalism limits one to shallow self-righteousness, and thus damns him.

Interestingly, Paul does not say, "Forbid the faithful to keep special days and special diets." Rather he says, "Do not let anyone judge you" in these things. (v. 16) There is great liberty in what we Christians can do: we can keep days and diets, or forget them. But he rejects the right of anyone to judge and/or compel another to comply with his own preferences. We are not to judge others by these things, and we are not to allow others to judge us. This is a warning to take to heart, because time and time again as legalism has come into the Church, the Church has become judgmental, joyless, uniform, and shallow in faith.

As bad as legalism is, there is another danger equally harmful — the sister error of mysticism.

"DO NOT LET ANYONE DISQUALIFY YOU": A WARNING AGAINST MYSTICISM (vv. 18, 19)

Before we explore this idea, we must say that Christian mysticism *per se* is not evil, for its goal is a deeper knowledge of God. What we are talking about here is a deceptive mysticism which is not rooted in Christ. In the context here, it is a mysticism derived from the pretense and imagination of the Gnostics. It bears some similarity to the pretense which Coach Johnny Kerr tried to get his Chicago Bulls to practice. As Kerr tells it:

> We had lost seven in a row, and I decided to give a psychological pep talk before the game with the Celtics. I told Bob Boozer to go out and pretend he was the best scorer in basketball. I told Jerry Sloan to pretend he was the best defensive guard. I told Guy Rodgers to pretend he could run an offense better than any other guard, and I told Eric Mueller to pretend he was the best rebounding, shot-blocking, scoring center in the game. We lost the game by 17. I was pacing around the locker room afterward trying to figure out what to say when Mueller walked up, put his arm around me and said, "Don't worry about it, coach. Just pretend we won."[2]

The Gnostics were great pretenders and fooled not only themselves, but the Colossians. Paul says that the Colossians were in danger of being deprived of their reward and future glory by the pretense of their cultured Gnostic friends.

> Do not let anyone who delights in false humility and the worship of angels disqualify you for the prize. Such a person goes into great detail about what he has seen, and his unspiritual mind puffs him up with idle notions. He has lost connection with the Head, from whom the whole body, supported and held together by its ligaments and sinews, grows as God causes it to grow. (vv. 18, 19)

The Gnostics' power to fool people came from their deceptive approach, which is delineated in the clauses of verse 18.

They used bogus humility, delighting in "false humility and the worship of angels." They loved to act humble and say, "We are not good enough to go directly to God, so we begin humbly with one of the angels, which, if we are in correct spirit, will elevate our requests through the hierarchy to God."

Next the Gnostic claimed to have special visions, going "into great detail about what he has seen." This was a technical phrase used in that day to describe "someone being admitted to a higher grade in one of the mystery religions."[3] Through this, they claimed to be on the inside. The Gnostic was actually proud. "His unspiritual mind puffs him up with idle notions," says Paul. Advertising humility, they were filled with huge conceit.

It was all vanity and sham, but learning the secrets of the spirit world can be enticing. Tarot cards, for example, are inviting. Their aesthetic design is meant to exude mystery, and millions have fallen into their lie. Likewise, the mystic signs of the Zodiac have claimed many. An exceptional display of piety is also attractive to many. Some people are drawn to those who say they are the "humblest" people in town. And the thought of being excluded from the "inner circle" is so devastating for some, they will do anything to get in.

C. S. Lewis, giving a guest lecture in 1944 to King's College (at the University of London), said that the desire to be in the inner circle (whatever it may be) is one of the "great permanent mainsprings of human action. Of all passions, the passion for the Inner Ring is most skillful in making a man who is not yet a very bad man do very bad things."[4] Applied to the realm of religion, this is especially true! Like the ancient dog of fable who, while carrying his bone, paused at seeing its own reflection in the water, and grabbing at the mirrored prize lost the one he had, there are multitudes who have lost *all* to deception.[5]

The root of the problem is laid bare in verse 19: "He has lost connection with the Head, from whom the whole body, supported and held together by its ligaments and sinews, grows as God causes it to grow." The false teachers had (and have) no part in the true Body of Christ. Conversely, this was (and is) the answer for those who want to steel themselves against their delusive teaching. We must hold fast to Christ, the Head.

> We drink of Thee, the Fountainhead,
> And thirst our souls from Thee to fill.
> (Bernard of Clairvaux)

LET NO ONE ENSLAVE YOU: A WARNING AGAINST ASCETICISM (vv. 20-23)

Spiritual discipline is good. But here Paul warns against extreme asceticism:

> Since you died with Christ to the basic principles of this world, why, as though you still belonged to it, do you submit to its rules: "Do not handle! Do not taste! Do not touch!"? These are all destined to perish with use, because they are based on human commands and teachings. Such regulations indeed have an

appearance of wisdom, with their self-imposed worship, their false humility and their harsh treatment of the body, but they lack any value in restraining sensual indulgence. (vv. 20-23)

Sadly, church history is replete with stories of ascetic excess in the rejection of beautiful and good things in the pursuit of God: rejection of marriage, sex, parenthood, the beauty of God's creation, even rejection of self. But this "self-made" religion does not do any good. In fact, it can heighten fleshly temptation and along with it produce a joyless, defensive approach to life.

Yet, surprisingly asceticism has its own seductiveness. Today, in its Eastern form, it attracts the indulgent, cultured elite. Thousands today have their gurus through whom they make their ascetic "nod-to-God." Seen for what it really is, this is an expression of independence from God which says, "I'm going to get to God on my own terms, by my own might." Asceticism feeds the flesh by starving it.[6]

The answer to such delusion is in the beginning of this section on asceticism, in verse 20: we have "died with Christ to the basic principles of this world." Our death in Christ has freed us from the "elemental spirits of the universe" (RSV), the demonic powers of this world which promote and thrive on human asceticism. Because we died with Christ, they have no actual power over us. We need to reckon this to our account (Romans 6:11, 12) and live in the full joy of God's creation, enjoying him and his people.

Paul has sounded a clear warning, calling us to look at things as they really are. Several years ago Royal Robbins, a professional mountain climber, wrote an article for *Sports Illustrated* which demonstrates the importance of seeing ourselves and life as we really are. He wrote:

If we are keenly alert and aware of the rock and what we are doing on it, if we are honest with ourselves and our capabilities and weaknesses, if we avoid committing ourselves beyond what we know is safe, then we will climb safely. For climbing is an exercise in reality. He who sees it clearly is on safe ground, regardless of his experience or skill. But he who sees reality as he would like it to be, may have his illusions rudely stripped from his eyes when the ground comes up fast.

The reality is this: "in Christ all the fullness of the Deity lives in bodily form," and in him we have been made full (2:9, 10). But we can lose the benefits of that fullness very easily. We can fall to *legalism* and its attendant self-righteousness, joylessness, and judgmentalism. We can succumb to *mysticism* and develop a proud, elitist spirit which contributes nothing to true worship. We can get into *asceticism*, thinking it will make us more holy, when actually it will feed our flesh.

The answer to legalism is the continual realization of the grace of Christ. The answer to mysticism is an understanding of how profoundly we are related to Christ. The answer to asceticism is the reckoning that we have died, been buried, and are resurrected with Christ. The answer is where it all began: at the foot of the Cross.

I have seen in my own life and the lives of those I have counseled that there is a tendency to move away from where we had our beginning: the Cross. All of our theology, all of our preaching, all of our singing hymns together, the disciplines of life experienced in family and relationships are meant to keep us right at the foot of the Cross—simply drinking long and deep from the Fountainhead, Jesus Christ.

11

The Seeking
of Things Above

COLOSSIANS 3:1-4

Paul has trumpeted his ancient warnings against evil teachings which would have robbed the Colossians of their wholeness in Christ. Now we see him provide a positive counterpart as he gives some coaching which will enhance the Colossians' fullness in Christ if it is taken to heart. His coaching will do the same for us, if we allow it, for although we are separated by 2,000 years, the human predicament is still the same, and the same advice still works.

When I was a boy growing up in the tennis-playing culture of Southern California, I learned that coaching can make all the difference. Those with the best mentors played best; those with good basic ability and the very best mentors could even become great. Coaching made the difference. Those who have heeded Paul's teaching have gone a long way, because it is instruction from God.

INSTRUCTIONS REGARDING OUR FULLNESS (vv. 1, 2)

"Since, then, you have been raised with Christ, set your heart on things above, where Christ is seated at the right hand of God." What are "things above"? Certainly they are not the physical things of Heaven, such as Christ's literal throne at the Father's right hand. Paul and the other apostles knew they were using figurative language. Luther railed at the erring artists of the Middle Ages, "Oh, that heaven of the charlatans, with its golden chair and Christ seated at the Father's side vested in a choir cope and a golden robe, as the painters love to portray Him!"[1] "Things above" were not material, but rather have to do with Christ's sovereign reign over the universe as he fills the universe with his power. They include his character, his presence, his heavenly joys. We are not to be seeking heavenly geography, but the One who dwells there.

Furthermore, the verb "set" is in the present imperative, which means a continuous, ongoing effort is required. We are to persistently seek and keep on seeking. Life abounds with examples of the persistence we are called to. Albert Einstein was dismissed from school in Munich because he was thought to lack interest in his studies. He next failed to pass an examination to enter a polytechnic school in Zurich. He became a tutor for the boys in a Zurich boarding house, but was soon fired. But he persisted over and over again, and you know how that story ended.[2]

Or consider the folklore about Lou Gehrig who, as an awkward rookie, was observed by Ty Cobb, who said, "Look at those piano legs — he'll never last." But with all his shortcomings, he set an all-time record of 2,130 consecutive games, the "Iron Man" of baseball.[3] Or there is the fabled record of archaeologist Howard Carter's monumental persistence through tons of rubble and discouragement and ridicule which eventuated in his finding the priceless tomb and treasure of Tutankhamen, King Tut. Such persistence is focused on rewards which, great as they are, cannot hold a candle to "things above." This heavenly seeking is to be foremost through prayer, as we ask, seek, and knock for the things above (Matthew 7:7; cf. Luke 18:1-5). This seeking ought to pervade our conversations, friendships, studies, work — even our play. And when it does, it will enhance our fullness in Christ.

The *act* of seeking depends upon the *set* of the mind: "Set your minds on things above, not on earthly things" (v. 2). As the story goes, penny-pinching Jack Benny was walking along when suddenly an armed robber approached and said, "Your money or your life!" There was a long pause as Benny did nothing. The robber impatiently cried, "Well?" Jack Benny replied, "Don't rush me! I'm thinking about it." Millions of people today think their things are their life. I once saw a poster which pictured a coffin with pallbearers and the deceased's possessions: a mansion, a helicopter, nine cars, including a Ferrari, a Rolls, an M.G., a Porsche, etc., with the caption: "He who has the most toys when he dies wins." For many, this is the philosophy of life. Sadly, many in the Church are not far behind:

> Theologies compete brazenly to rationalize wealth, success and material blessing. Prosperity doctrines gush forth from rallies, radio and television. ("God's got it, I can have it, and by faith I'm

going to get it.") Even Psalm 23 has been revised ("The Lord is my banker, my credit is good. He giveth me the key to his strong-box. He restoreth my faith in riches. He guideth me in the paths of prosperity for his name's sake.")[4]

People today spend not because they need, but for identity.

Paul says in response that we are *not* to set our minds "on earthly things." This includes not only material possessions, but the immaterial things of this world: earthly honors, position, advancement. We must note that Paul is not suggesting that the Christian withdraw from commerce and any possibility of prominence or achievement. Taken to absurdity, there would never be a Christian surgeon or chef; there would be no excellence. The difference is that the Christian is no longer to see these things as if they are all that matter. Moreover, his mind-set is to be dominated by "things above." Paul is precise in his command: "Set your minds on things above" and keep it that way. Implicit here is the idea of concentration.

I recently played catch with a little dog named Bozie. After spending forty-five minutes tossing the ball for Bozie, I concluded that when she dies an autopsy will reveal she has a tennis ball for a brain! Bozie sleeps with her tennis ball, carries it to her water dish, and can find it wherever it is thrown. Her mind is constantly set on the tennis ball. So it should be with us regarding "things above."

We see in these verses the "Great Divide" in the Christian life. What we set our minds on determines our seeking and thus the direction of our Christian lives. What do you think about when you have nothing else to do? Some common-sense qualifications are in order here, because we all variously daydream about our favorite team or a coming vacation or our yard. Sometimes we are under such pressures at home or work that we can scarcely think of anything else. But these things aside, do our minds regularly go up to Christ and "things above"? If they do not, we are in trouble. The Bible says, "For where your treasure is, there your heart will be also" (Luke 12:34; cf. Matthew 6:21). What will the divine post-mortem reveal to be our highest priority? A dress? A fishing pole? Christ?

This mind-set begins with prayer: "Lord, set my mind on things above." Jesus said, "If you remain in me and my words remain in you, ask whatever you wish, and it will be given you" (John 15:7).

We must also remember that our mind-set is a deliberate act of the will. We set our minds on taking a vacation. We set our minds on buying an object. We set our minds on finishing a project. We can set our minds on "things above."

In addition, we need to hold loosely to the things below, our possessions. Remember the parable of the rich young ruler who came to Jesus asking what he must do to inherit eternal life. Jesus told him to sell all he had, and the man went away sorrowing. The truth is, every one of us *is* that rich, young ruler. Every one of us has incredible wealth — more things than we know what to do with. Because of our possessions, it is difficult to set our minds on things above. There are two ways to hold something: with a clenched fist or with an open hand. A good exercise for each of us is to learn to regularly give something away which we value very much.

Finally, it is immensely helpful to memorize Scriptures which have to do with a heavenly mind-set, such as Colossians 3:1-4, Ephesians 1 and 2, or 2 Corinthians 12:1-4. Follow the advice above, and the fullness of Christ will be perpetual and growing — and no one will be able to rob you of it.

THE REASONING BEHIND PAUL'S INSTRUCTIONS (vv. 3, 4)

Paul's reasoning is based on the *past* and *future* history of all true believers. Our *past* is given in verse 3: "For you died, and your life is now hidden with Christ in God." We actually died when we were baptized into the Body of Christ by the Holy Spirit (1 Corinthians 12:13; Romans 6:1-5). Thus, our life was "hidden with Christ in God." The tense here is imperfect, which stresses ongoing effects. Our lives have been hidden with Christ's, and they remain that way. Because we are in Christ and Christ is in God, we are inseparable and secure. Our lives are a part of the "above." The world without Christ does not understand the source of our life in him. There is something genuine about the believer which will tax the brightest intelligence to explain. In him there is fullness. His fullness has passed into our emptiness, his righteousness into our sinfulness, his life into our death.

Our *future* is described in verse 4: "When Christ, who is your life, appears, then you also will appear with him in glory." Right now our lives are hidden in Christ, but when he is revealed at his coming in his glorious body, we will also be revealed because we will have bodies like his. Paul describes this in Philippians 3:20, 21 — "But our citizenship is in heaven. And we eagerly await a Savior from there, the Lord Jesus Christ, who, by the power that enables him to bring everything under his control, will transform our lowly bodies so that they will be like his glorious body." Then we will be revealed! Those without Christ cannot now understand this, but then it will be perfectly clear. So sure is this that Paul speaks in Romans 8:29-31 as if it has already happened:

> For those God foreknew he also predestined to be conformed to the likeness of his Son, that he might be the firstborn among many brothers. And those he predestined, he also called; those he

called, he also justified; those he justified, he also glorified. What, then, shall we say in response to this? If God is for us, who can be against us?

What a spectacular future awaits us!

Let us covenant to not fix our thoughts on the material and immaterial things of this world, but to pray for minds set on things above, to hold the Scriptures close to our hearts, to reflect on our past history, and to rejoice in anticipation of our future in him.

12

The Putting Off,
Putting On (I)

COLOSSIANS 3:5-11

In Paul's writing, theology is always followed by a call to live it out. For example, in the book of Ephesians, the first three chapters are given to highest theology, only to be followed with this practical call in 4:1 — "As a prisoner for the Lord, then, I urge you to live a life worthy of the calling you have received." This call introduces the remainder of the book. Similarly, the magisterial theology of Romans 1 – 11 culminates in this great doxology: "For from him and through him and to him are all things. To him be the glory forever! Amen" (11:36). This is followed by a most practical call: "Therefore, I urge you, brothers, in view of God's mercy, to offer your bodies as living sacrifices" (12:1).

We have the same thing here in Colossians, where the sublimely esoteric theology of Chapters 1 and 2 spawns the challenge in 3:5 — "Put to death, therefore, whatever belongs to your earthly nature." For Paul, doctrine demands duty; creed determines conduct; facts demand acts.

We will now begin to study the practical application of the vast theology we have already studied.

LAYING ASIDE THE OLD LIFE: THE CHALLENGE (vv. 5-9a)

> Put to death, therefore, whatever belongs to your earthly nature: sexual immorality, impurity, lust, evil desires and greed, which is idolatry. Because of these, the wrath of God is coming. You used to walk in these ways, in the life you once lived. (vv. 5-7)

95

Jesus spoke of this same idea when he said: "If your right eye causes you to sin, gouge it out and throw it away" (Matthew 5:29). Obviously neither Paul nor Jesus was recommending literal surgery, for sin does not come from the eye (or the hand), but from the heart — the evil within. Centuries past in England, if a pickpocket was caught and convicted, his right hand was cut off. If he was caught again, his left hand suffered the same fate. One pickpocket lost both hands and continued his occupation with his teeth![1] Physical dismemberment cannot change the heart. "Put to death," as Paul uses it, means to discard evil practices and, here in Colossians, to get rid of the twin evils of sexual sin and covetousness.

Specifically, there are four elements of sinful sensuality which must be executed. The first is "immorality" (*porneian*), from which we get the word *pornographic*. It means every kind of immoral sexual relation. Chastity was the one completely new virtue which Christianity brought to the world.[2] Paul's call was radical to the pagan culture in its day, and it is almost as radical today. As you voice Biblical morality, you often will be labeled a moral brontosaurus! The second element of sensuality which we are to kill is "impurity," moral uncleanness. This is wider and subtler than physical immorality, for it embraces the lurid imagination, speech, and deed of a sensual heart or filthy mind. The third element is "lust," the shameful emotion which leads to sexual excesses. Paul used the same word to describe the "passionate lust" of the Gentiles who do not know God (1 Thessalonians 4:5) and the "shameful lusts" of homosexuality (Romans 1:26). The fourth element of sensuality to be discarded is "evil desires" — wicked, self-serving, rapacious lust. What a deadly quartet we have here, and Paul said it must be slain outright — executed!

Personally I can think of no other array of sins more prominent in our society — and more in need of being put away. Daily living subjects the average American to a sea of sensuality. It is conceivable that on a given evening of TV watching, one may see more sensual sights than one's grandparents did in their lifetimes. The magazine ads for certain brands of blue jeans defy adequate description in polite company, and the Fellini-inspired TV ads for perfume promote a mystical eroticism. The January 1984 issue of *Psychology Today*, a magazine not known for promoting Biblical concern, stated that a pervasive cultural desensitization has taken place through films which feature sexual violence, and suggested that such films be packaged with warning labels (as are cigarettes)!

What makes the situation even worse is the amazing human capacity for self-delusion in respect to sensuality. I have known professing, Bible-carrying "Christians" who talked sensitively about theology and serious issues, yet were adulterous and even incestuous. I have known Christian workers who were fundamentalists at work (mouthing all the shibboleths) and cable TV voyeurs at home. Even more tragic, the delusion is so deep that they see no inconsistency in their behavior.

Regardless of man's delusion, God's Word still speaks: "Put to death, therefore, whatever belongs to your earthly nature: sexual immorality, impurity, lust, evil desires." This is a violent metaphor which expresses pain and effort. Killing naturally means tears and blood, but here it means even more. As Alexander Maclaren said: "It is far easier to cut off the hand, which after all is not me, than to sacrifice passions and desires which, though they be my worst self, are myself."[3]

This metaphor teaches us that we must execute sensuality whatever the cost! Proverbs 6:27 says, "Can a man scoop fire into his lap without his clothes being burned?" Many Christians are daily heaping fire onto themselves and are being profoundly scarred. We need to be like Job, who said, "I made a covenant with my eyes not to look lustfully at a girl" (Job 31:1). We need to apply this across the board. There are books and magazines we must discard. Some of us need to toss out TVs. I am not endorsing any type of legalism, but God's Word speaks today, and we are to kill the members of our body which lead us into sensuality or promote covetousness, which our text calls "greed, which is idolatry."

The word "greed" or "covetousness" (KJV) which Paul used here denotes not merely the desire to possess more than one has, but more than one ought to have, particularly that which belongs to someone else.[4] The mention of this at the end of a list of sexual sins is highly significant, for it is intimately associated with them. It is really another form of the same evil desire, except that it is fixed on material things. Often when sensuality loses its hold, materialism takes its place. In my opinion, this is why many middle-aged men who were once devoted to sensuality are now equally given to money. These sins have the same source. Such greed is really the lowest form of idolatry, for nothing could be lower than putting our trust in a material thing and making that our god.

Whatever I put my trust in, I worship. Materialism is the true religion of thousands of confessing Christians today. There is a sense in which covetousness is even more dangerous than sensuality, because it has so many respectable forms. So often it is the successful covetous person whom we honor. As the proverb goes: If a man is drunk with wine, we kick him out of the church; if he is drunk with money, we make him a deacon!

This is serious business, because both these sins provoke the wrath of God: "Because of these, the wrath of God is coming. You used to walk in these ways, in the life you once lived" (vv. 6, 7). Paul's message is clear: since we have died, and have been buried, resurrected, and ascended with Christ, since we have been made full of his fullness, there are some things we must put off: namely, sensuality and materialism. We arᴜ to slay them, regardless of the blood and the pain!

We are also to put off evil attitudes and speech: "But now you must rid yourselves of all such things as these: anger, rage, malice, slander, and filthy language from your lips. Do not lie to each other" (vv. 8, 9a). It is said that Jonathan Edwards, third president of Princeton and America's greatest thinker, had a daughter with an ungovernable temper. As is often the case, the problem was not known to the outside world. A young man fell in love with this daughter and sought her hand in marriage.

"You can't have her," was the abrupt answer of Jonathan Edwards.

"But I love her," the young man replied.

"You can't have her," said Edwards.

"But she loves me," replied the young man.

Again Edwards said, "You can't have her."

"Why?" asked the young man.

"Because she is not worthy of you."

"But," he asked, "she is a Christian, is she not?"

"Yes, she is a Christian, but the grace of God can live with some people with whom no one else could ever live."[5]

So it is with the believer filled with "anger, rage, malice." The "anger" described here is growing, inner anger, like sap in a tree on a hot day which swells the trunk and branches until they are in danger of bursting. "Rage" is that anger boiling over. We see it in a quick temper. "Malice" bespeaks a viciousness of mind. It is the malignant attitude which plans evil and rejoices when misery falls on the one it hates, like Haman's glee in building the gallows for Mordecai (Esther 5:14). These evil attitudes must be put away. If they are not, "the heated metal of anger will be forged into poisoned arrows of the tongue."[6] Further, "slander" will follow — that is, hurtful speech which defames one's character. This, unchecked, will turn into "filthy language from your lips" — foul, obscene, abusive speech. Do not naively suppose that such things do not exist among professing believers. They do! "The grace of God can live with some people with whom no one else could ever live."

Paul continued, "Do not lie to each other" (v. 9a). Lying is a great sin against God, against the Church, and against love. That is why God struck down Ananias and Sapphira in the first church. He wanted truth, not deception, not hypocrisy. "Therefore each of you must put off falsehood and speak truthfully to his neighbor, for we are all members of one body" (Ephesians 4:25). A great church demands great honesty.

LAYING ASIDE THE OLD LIFE: THE RATIONALE (vv. 9b-ll)

Paul's reason for living a godly life was this: ". . . since you have taken off your old self with its practices and have put on the new self, which is being renewed in knowledge in the image of its Creator" (vv. 9b, 10). We must put off the evil practices of our former life because when we came to Christ, being baptized into his body (1 Corinthians 12:13) and born again (John 3:5-7), we spiritually "took off the old self" and "put on the new self." "Therefore, if anyone is in Christ, he is a new creation the old has gone, the new has come" (2 Corinthians 5:17). All authentic believers have a new self, with new spiritual sensitivities and abilities, and thus wonderfully new possibilities in this life.

This "new self . . . is being renewed in knowledge in the image of its Creator" (v. 10). There is constant renewal taking place in the believer's life as he keeps increasing in true knowledge of what God is like. This knowledge leads to progressively being conformed to the image of the Creator, and thus building a life like his. What a thought! Paul says similarly in 2 Corinthians 4:16, "Therefore we do not lose heart. Though outwardly we are wasting away, yet inwardly we are being renewed day by day." And again, in 2 Corinthians 3:18, "And we, who with unveiled faces all reflect the Lord's glory, are being transformed into his likeness with ever-increasing glory, which comes from the Lord, who is the Spirit." The more we put off the old nature, the greater freedom we have for the renewal of our new self according to the image of God.

The final reason for putting off the evils of the old self is that the new self brings a renewal that is so radical, it changes all human relationships. Paul says in verse 11: "Here there is no Greek or Jew, circumcised or uncircumcised, barbarian, Scythian, slave or free, but Christ is all, and is in all." If we make a practice of putting to death our sensuality and covetousness, laying aside evil attitudes and malignant speech, we will fully experience this astounding removal of barriers in human relationships. The "new self," lived out, brings the destruction of *racial* barriers ("Greek or Jew"), *religious* barriers ("circumcised or uncircumcised"), *cultural* barriers ("barbarian, Scythian"), and *social* barriers ("slave or free"). This will bring a resounding affirmation of Tertullian's exclamation: "See how these Christians love one another!"[7] An amazed world will acknowledge that Christians have the "real thing": "All men will know that you are my disciples if you love one another" (John 13:35).

As in Paul's letters to the Romans and the Ephesians, the high theology of Colossians 1 and 2 demands immense application. We must put off:

- *Sensuality* — "sexual immorality, impurity, lust, evil desires and greed."

- *Evil attitudes* — "anger, rage, malice."
- *Evil speech* — "slander, filthy language."
- *Deception* — "do not lie to each other."

Why must we put these things off? Because we have:

- *A new self* "which is being renewed in knowledge in the image of its Creator."
- *New relationships* — "Here there is no Greek or Jew . . . but Christ is all, and is in all."

What motivation to put off the old and put on the new!

13

The Putting Off, Putting On (II)

COLOSSIANS 3:12-14

The apostle began a new section with a welcome and a soothing description of believers: "God's chosen people, holy and dearly loved." What is remarkable is that each of these three titles was an honored Old Testament apellation for Israel, "God's chosen people." "The Lord did not set his affection on you and *choose* you because you were more numerous than other peoples, for you were the fewest of all peoples. But it was because the Lord *loved* you" (Deuteronomy 7:7, 8a emphasis mine). The Colossians were now chosen by God and thus were secure. "Who will bring any charge against those whom God has chosen? It is God who justifies" (Romans 8:33). Israel also had been designated "holy" — that is, set apart for God himself. These Colossians were now given that august title. And, most beautifully, Israel was called "dearly loved." These Colossian believers now wore this title with all its privileges and rights.

What a rich array of titles! These opulent apellations were meant to soothe the Colossian believers' Gentile Christian hearts and prepare them for the great putting on which was immediately commanded. In these verses the Colossians were commanded to put on virtues which stood in brilliant contrast to the vices which the Colossians were previously commanded to put off. Here we have the wardrobe of the saints, and what beautiful garments they are!

PUTTING ON SAINTS' CLOTHING (v. 12)

"Therefore, as God's chosen people, holy and dearly loved, clothe your-selves with compassion, kindness, humility, gentleness and patience." The first article of clothing is "compassion." The old *King James Version* ren-ders this more literally, "bowels of mercies" because the word literally refers to the stomach or entrails, where so much of our emotion is felt. Peter O'Brien says that this term forcefully expressed personality at the deepest level, especially in the matter of living.[1] A good translation might be, "tenderness of heart" or "tender mercies."

The ancient world, apart from Biblical revelation, was merciless. The maimed and sickly and aged were discarded; the mentally ill were subjected to inhumanities. But Christianity brought compassion, and it still does. "It is not too much," says William Barclay, "to say that every-thing that has been done for the aged, the sick, the weak in body and in mind, the animal, the child, the woman has been done under the inspira-tion of Christianity."[2] The gospel brings with it sympathy and tenderness of heart. That is one of its great glories!

Paul is telling us here that if we are new creatures in Christ, we must be compassionate people. John Perkins, in his book *Let Justice Roll Down*, tells about a time of dark, extended discouragement in his life when he was ill and seriously thinking of giving up the struggle. Then he met a Dr. Roberts. In Perkins's words: "Dr. Roberts was one of the few white persons I had contact with at that time, and she—well, she met me on the level of my humanity and not just on the theological level pre-ferred by so many church folks."[3] Dr. Roberts saw him through his great crisis with her merciful compassion. This is something of what we are called to—every one of us! All of us must be tenderly merciful. This is the first garment.

The second item of clothing is simply "kindness." Kindness does not happen naturally in human relationships. George Bernard Shaw once wrote a letter to Churchill: "Enclosed are two tickets to the opening night of my first play . . . bring a friend (if you have one)." Churchill replied: "Dear Mr. Shaw, unfortunately I'll be unable to attend the opening night of your play due to a prior engagement. Please send me tickets for a sec-ond night (if you have one)." We should probably understand that there is considerable playfulness by these words. But the human personality natu-rally descends to harshness in word and deed.

The great Archbishop Trench, the prime mover behind the *Oxford English Dictionary*, says that the Greek word here translated "kindness" is a lovely word for a lovely quality. It was used to describe wine which has grown mellow with age and has lost its harshness.[4] It was used by

Jesus to describe his yoke: "My yoke is easy" (Matthew 11:30). It is listed in Galatians 5:22 as a fruit of the Spirit, and thus is a result of the fullness of God in human life. It is a quality of God himself, for Romans 2:4 tells us that God's "kindness" leads us to repentance. Kindness is an altogether lovely article of clothing.

The third garment we are to don is that of "humility," a word the Greeks never applied to themselves. William Gladstone, the learned prime minister of England, once remarked to his scholarly peer John Morley: "It is a pathetic reflection that while humility is the sovereign grace of Christianity, the Greeks had no symbol in their language to denote it. Every word akin to it has in it some element of meanness, feebleness, or contempt."[5] But the gospel took this word of contempt and made it one of its chief graces. It was used to describe Christ's humbling himself by becoming obedient to death (Philippians 2:8). Christians are called to serve God (Acts 20:19) and one another (Ephesians 4:2) with all humility and lowliness. Jesus himself invited his followers to learn from him, as he was lowly in heart (Matthew 11:29).

Jesus was *not* suggesting a cringing, groveling servility; nor was he teaching his followers to think poorly of themselves. Rather, he was teaching the necessity of the absence of self-exaltation. He wanted us to have nothing of the arrogant pride that Churchill evidently saw in his antagonist Sir Stafford Cripps when he remarked as Cripps walked by: "There, but for the grace of God, goes God." The person who wears the garment of humility knows who God is, what man is, and who he or she is. Those who walk with awareness through a wheat field will notice that it is the drooping ears that are heavy with grain. Humility is a proper garment for every believer.

The fourth item with which we are to clothe ourselves is "gentleness," or as the older translations have it, "meekness."[6] Some time ago humorist J. Upton Dickson said he was writing a book titled *Cower Power*, and that he had also founded a group for submissive people called DOORMATS, which stands for: "Dependent Organization Of Really Meek And Timid Souls — if there are no objections." Their motto is, "The meek shall inherit the earth — if that's okay with everybody." Their symbol is the yellow traffic light.[7] Mr. Dickson has a clever sense of humor, but the misconception he exploits is no laughing matter, for most people think that meekness/gentleness is weakness. Nothing could be farther from the truth.

There is gentleness and self-effacement in this word, but behind the gentleness is a steel-like strength, for the supreme characteristic of the meek man or woman is that he or she is under perfect control. Gentleness/meekness is strength under control. Numbers 12:3 tells us that

Moses was the most "meek" (KJV) man on earth, but at the same time Moses was a man who could act decisively, be as hard as nails, and rise in anger at the proper time.[8] Those wearing the true garment of gentleness/meekness are immensely powerful people, for they are controlled by God.

The final garment from the celestial closet is "patience," long-suffering in the face of insult or injury. This is one of the fruits of the Spirit (Galatians 5:22), and it means more than just enduring difficulties or passive resignation to the circumstances. It is based on a lively, outgoing faith in God and is to be exercised toward "everyone," as Paul instructs us in 1 Thessalonians 5:14. It is an excellent garment, to be sure.

So we have Heaven's wardrobe from the hand of the Ultimate Tailor. It is revealing to note, as many have before, that all of these garments were perfectly worn by Christ. Therefore, when we put on these five graces, we are putting on a family resemblance to Christ.

> *I want the adorning divine*
> *Thou only, my God, can bestow,*
> *I want in those beautiful garments to shine*
> *Which distinguish Thy household below.*[9]

One other fact about this wardrobe: all these garments can be worn only in community with others, in relationships. How tempting to think that these garments would be so much easier to wear if we did not have to wear them among people. How much easier to *think* about "compassion" than to *do* it. How much easier to be kind when we are away from mean people. It would be far easier to put on "humility" and "gentleness" if we were not being jostled by the proud and assertive. How much easier "patience" is in isolation. But that is not the way it works! Christians become better Christians in community, in their families, among their associates, in their dorms, in their churches, where there is sweat and breath. The truth is: the very things we may think are keeping us from putting on these garments are the things which make possible their wearing. "Clothe yourselves" is a present imperative: "Put them on and keep putting them on."

WEARING SAINTS' CLOTHING (v. 13)

What will happen when we don this marvelous attire? ". . . bearing with one another, and forgiving each other, whoever has a complaint against anyone; just as the Lord forgave you, so also should you" (NASB) Wearing saintly attire promotes the capacity to "bear with each other." That is no small accomplishment! In the days before smoking sections on planes, a passenger started to light a cigar when the stewardess informed him that cigar smoking was not allowed unless it was alright with the other person in the immediate area. "Do you object to his smoking?" she asked the woman seated next to the man. "I absolutely detest cigars," was the stony reply. The stewardess then spoke to a young man near the front of the cabin and came back to report that he would not mind sitting next to a cigar smoker. As the cigar-smoking man walked forward to his new seat, his former seatmate, the boisterous woman, turned to the stewardess and confided, "I've been married to that man for thirty years, and I still can't stand his awful cigars." This is a humorous example of how closely related people — family — often relate (or fail to relate) to each other. Further, it is a parable of what all too frequently happens in God's family.

> To live above with the saints we love,
> Oh, that will be glory.
> But to live below with the saints we know,
> Well, that's another story.

The Church is the place where people must bear with one another in love. Paul tells us in Ephesians 2:10 that we are Christ's "workmanship," or more literally, "his masterwork." We are in process, and ultimately we will be masterpieces, though it may be difficult to perceive it now. We are not yet what we are going to be, and we need to "bear with one another" as the process goes on.

Inevitably this mutual forbearing must extend to mutual forgiving: "forgive whatever grievances you may have against one another. Forgive as the Lord forgave you" (v. 13). Forgiveness has never been in vogue. Primitive Lamech strutted before his wives and gave this chest-thumping speech: "[L]isten to me; wives of Lamech, hear my words. I have killed a man for wounding me, a young man for injuring me. If Cain is avenged seven times, then Lamech seventy-seven times" (Genesis 4:23, 24). "If God avenges himself only seven times, I will do it seventy-seven times!" Similarly, the colonial General Oglethorpe is reported to have raged at John Wesley, "I never forgive." Though many people retain the poison of hatred in their lives, forgiveness is commanded and is possible through Christ.

John Perkins tells how he was beaten in a Mississippi jail, being repeatedly kicked and stomped on as he lay in a fetal position for protection. The beating went on and on as he writhed in a pool of his own blood while inebriated officers took turns, using their feet and blackjacks. At one point an officer took an unloaded pistol, put it to Perkins's head, and pulled the trigger. Then another bigger man beat him until he was unconscious. As the night wore on, it got worse. During a conscious period, one officer pushed a fork down his throat.[10] It was barbarous torture, a great, substantive reason to hate. But this is what happened, as John Perkins tells it:

> The Spirit of God worked on me as I lay in that bed. An image formed in my mind. The image of the cross—Christ on the cross. It blotted out everything else in my mind. This Jesus knew what I had suffered. He understood. And He cared. Because He had experienced it all Himself. This Jesus, this One who had brought good news directly from God in heaven, had lived what He preached. Yet He was arrested and falsely accused. Like me, He went through an unjust trial. He also faced a lynch mob and got beaten. But even more than that, He was nailed to rough wooden planks and killed. Killed like a common criminal. At the crucial moment, it seemed to Jesus that even God Himself had deserted Him. The suffering was so great, He cried out in agony. He was dying. But when He looked at that mob who had lynched Him, He didn't hate them. He loved them. He forgave them. And He prayed God to forgive them. "Father, forgive these people, for they don't know what they are doing." His enemies hated. But Jesus forgave. I couldn't get away from that. . . . It's a profound, mysterious truth—Jesus' concept of love overpowering hate. I may not see its victory in my lifetime. But I know it's true. I know it's true, because it happened to me. On that bed, full of bruises and stitches—God made it true in me. He washed my hatred away and replaced it with a love for the white man in rural Mississippi. I felt strong again. Stronger than ever. What doesn't destroy me makes me stronger. I know it's true. Because it happened to me.[11]

"Forgive as the Lord forgave you." It is not enough to put up with each other, to refuse retaliation—we must truly forgive. And if we struggle with this, we must, as did John Perkins, recall the immense forgiveness of Christ.

THE ULTIMATE SAINTLY GARMENT (v. 14)

"And over all these virtues put on love, which binds them all together in perfect unity." The apostle envisions a man dressing his body with the flowing garments of the day, and then it occurs to the man that as beautiful and fine as his garments are, they can never be worn with comfort or grace until they are held in place by a belt. So he adds the belt: "love." It is possible to have some of the five recommended garments and not have love, but it is impossible to have love and not have all of the five garments. Bruce calls love "the grace that binds all these other graces together."[12] And that it is. The imperative thrust is continuous: keep putting on love over and over and over again.

May we never neglect "love, which binds them all together in perfect unity."

14

The Fullness of His Peace, Word, and Name

COLOSSIANS 3:15-17

This chapter's text deals with the pleasurable commands which come to the child of God who has put off the old self and put on the new. Specifically, these commands touch on the fullness of Christ's *peace* (v. 15), the fullness of his *word* (v. 16), and the fullness of his *name* (v. 17).

R. E. O. White, the British preacher, observed regarding the fullness which these verses command: "The surest sign that you are carrying a full bucket is wet feet." That is true to our experience, is it not? Whenever we attempt to carry a full bucket to clean the floor or wash the car, we *always* get wet feet! And when our lives are full, they *will* overflow.

THE FULLNESS OF HIS PEACE (v. 15)

"Let the peace of Christ rule in your hearts, since as members of one body you were called to peace. And be thankful." What is this peace like?

I can still remember my first experience of this peace. Though I was not quite a teenager, I knew my sins were separating me from God. I had been under deep conviction for several months, for I had been attending a church where the gospel was very clearly preached. I knew that I was on the outside of the mysteries of spiritual life, and I wanted in. Finally one night, in a rustic chapel high in the Sierra-Nevada Mountains, I met Christ. I yet remember the aroma of that room, the cedar and the redwood, the expression of the man who talked with me, and the initial fullness of Christ's peace. It saturated my whole being!

That night after "lights out," I scooted down in my sleeping bag and switched on my flashlight. There I opened the tiny India-paper Bible which my grandmother had given me when I was seven years old and reread the verses that I had underlined in the chapel that night. The peace of God surged over me again and again. I was at peace with God and the world!

"The peace of Christ" is different from any other kind. In the brief hours before he died, Jesus said to his disciples, "Peace I leave with you; my peace I give you. I do not give to you as the world gives" (John 14:27). He gives us a special peace which he calls "my peace." He gives us his own *personal* peace. It is not just the peace we experience when there is no conflict. It is a sense of wholeness and well-being, completeness and totality. But it is even more — it is the *presence* of Christ. His peace and his presence are marvelously associated in both the Old and New Testament Scriptures (see, for example, Numbers 6:24-26). It was his presence that was with me in the chapel and in my grubby sleeping bag! It is this experience of peace — the cessation of hostility with God, the sense of well-being, and the sense of his presence — that has marked my life.

What are we to do with this peace? "Let the peace of Christ rule in your hearts." What does that mean? F. F. Bruce, the New Testament scholar to whom we owe so much, says "rule" carried the idea of "arbitrate."[1] In many extra-Biblical sources, the Greek word used here referred to the function of one who took it on himself to decide what is right in a contest. The sense here is, "Let the peace of Christ be umpire in your heart amidst the conflicts of life. Let it decide what is right. Let it be your counselor."

An old story which comes from the Salvation Army in the last century tells of a strong-willed woman who had been nicknamed "Warrior Brown" because of her fiery temper. She was often belligerent and became enraged whenever she got drunk. Then one day she was converted. Her entire life was wonderfully changed by the indwelling presence of the Holy Spirit. At an open-air meeting a week later, she told everyone what Jesus had done for her. Suddenly a scoffer threw a potato at her, causing a stinging bruise. Had she not been converted, she would have lashed out at the man furiously. God's grace, however, had made such a profound change in her conduct that she quietly picked up the potato and put it into her pocket without saying a word. No more was heard of the incident until the time of the "harvest festival" months later. Then the dear lady who had been known as "Warrior Brown" brought as her offering a little sack of potatoes. She explained that after the open-air meeting she had cut up and planted the "insulting potato," and what she was now presenting to the Lord was "the increase." Warrior Brown had allowed "the peace of Christ" to be umpire of her life.

How much misery we would avoid if we permitted "the peace of Christ" to umpire in our hearts. How many words we would hold back if he were the arbitrator in our lives. How many sleepless nights we would forego if we did that. How the Church needs this too, "since as members of one body you were called to peace."

Paul concludes his exhortation in verse 15 by saying, "And be thankful," a command repeated at the ends of verses 16 and 17. When the buckets we carry are full of Christ, our lives are bathed with the peace of God in thanksgiving.

THE FULLNESS OF HIS WORD (v. 16)

> Let the word of Christ dwell in you richly as you teach and
> admonish one another with all wisdom, and as you sing psalms,
> hymns and spiritual songs with gratitude in your hearts to God.

How can we allow the Word of God to dwell richly among us? We must begin by reading it. The Bible is not all that hard to understand, though there are admittedly some very difficult passages. Mark Twain put it in perspective when he said, "Most people are bothered by those passages of Scripture which they cannot understand; but as for me, I have always noticed that the passages in Scripture which trouble me most are those which I do understand." The Bible is understandable, and we need to read it. We need to be both comforted and troubled by it, as is appropriate to each of our lives.

We must also realize that reading does not guarantee that the Word of Christ will "dwell" in us "richly." The parallel quotation in Ephesians 5:18, 19, which lists the *same* results from the filling of the Spirit, teaches us that God's Word must be read and meditated on under the influence of the Holy Spirit if it is to dwell richly in us. Richness comes when, as we are yielded to the Holy Spirit, we meditate upon short passages, memorize others, and then do what they say. It is not just a question of disciplined study. It is a matter of the heart. It is Spirit-filled participation in Christ and his Word. And is it ever rich!

That night when I was deep in my sleeping bag, with flashlight on, turning the pages of my Bible with my grimy fingers, reading verse after verse, the Word of God was dwelling richly within me. There was music in my unmusical soul.

My experience of this richness perfectly accords with how Paul says it manifests itself — ". . . as you teach and admonish one another with all wisdom, and as you sing psalms, hymns and spiritual songs with gratitude in your hearts to God." This also accounts for Tertullian's second-century description of a Christian love feast at which "after water for the hands and lights have been brought in, each is invited to sing to God in the presence of the others from his own heart."[2] It is the telltale sign of the richly indwelling Word.

Imagine the Early Church. One got up and sang perhaps from a psalm, and another answered antiphonally. Hymns broke forth in hearty chorus. Others sang spontaneously about what God had done. There was music in their hearts. That is what this verse is talking about. You can find this repeated in church history. The record of Christian awakenings during the last 2,000 years shows that whenever the Word of God is recovered, it is received with great joy which is inevitably expressed in song. The medieval Latin hymns cluster around the fresh days of the monastic movements. The Protestant Reformation brought a rebirth of music to the Church. When we think of the Wesleyan Revival, we not only think of John Wesley, but his brother Charles who has given us so many great hymns. The great harvest of souls here in our own country in the late 1960s and 1970s brought a revival of Scripture singing. When the Word of God dwells richly within you, you want to sing "with gratitude in your hearts to God."

As a new Christian, I sang those old gospel hymns with all I had. And so it has been whenever my heart is right with God. When the buckets of our lives are full to the brim with God's Word, we cannot move without spilling forth in song. Music is the window of the soul. How is it in our souls?

THE FULLNESS OF HIS NAME (v. 17)

> And whatever you do, whether in word or deed, do it all in the name of the Lord Jesus, giving thanks to God the Father through him.

There are few exhortations in Scripture that are more comprehensive than this one. "Word or deed" takes in everything in life. "Deeds" can be preaching, teaching, eating, exercising, driving, cleaning house, shopping, visiting, working, playing (basketball, soccer, tennis, fishing, even watching) — everything! Our words are everything that passes our lips, even in unguarded moments. *Everything* we say or do is to be done "in the name of the Lord Jesus."

Our actions must say that Jesus is and does exactly what he claims! Just a few seconds of sin can disgrace the greatest of names. The Hebrew name *Judah* means "praise"; the New Testament equivalent is *Judas*. When our lives are full of Christ, praise to his name in word and deed floods our paths, bringing refreshment to all. What a responsibility is ours!

The fullness of Christ comes from an overflow of his *peace* and his *word* and his *name*. It is also seen in our thankfulness. Verse 15 ends with, "And be thankful." Verse 16 concludes with, "gratitude in your hearts to God." Verse 17 says, "giving thanks to God the Father through him."

The most direct of these exhortations to thankfulness is in verse 15, "And be thankful." Literally it says, "become thankful," because we are to keep on striving for a deeper gratitude than we have yet attained. The word for "thankful" is the word *eucharesteo*, from which we get the English word *Eucharist*, another word for the Lord's Supper — a time for giving thanks.

Full pails cannot help but overflow. May each day result in deep thanksgiving.

15

The Christian Family (I)

COLOSSIANS 3:18, 19

We have considered the cosmic fullness of Christ who created and presently sustains the universe by his power. We have also examined the implications of his fullness for every area of life. Now we will look at the *domestic fullness* of Christ. In the earlier studies we saw the cosmic, supra-mundane; here all is domestic and totally mundane. We move from the religion of the universe to the religion of the kitchen and bedroom. Since Christ is the fullness of the universe, he must also be the source of fullness in the home.

Colossians 3:18 – 4:1 could well be titled, "How to Have a Full, Rich Family Life." The text contains three sets of exhortations: verses 18 and 19 to wives and husbands, verses 20 and 21 to children and parents, 3:22 – 4:1 to servants and masters.

Colossians 3:18, 19 is patently domestic. It has to do with *home*, specifically a Christian home. Moreover, it has to do with the relationship between a *Christian* husband and a *Christian* wife. As such, it has nothing to say about men's and women's roles in society, such as the marketplace or politics. There are other texts which give us some guidance in these areas, but we do Scripture a great disservice by applying it where it was never intended. The teaching here is for Christians who want to live as Christians within the home and experience all the fullness God intended for them. It is teaching which is much needed today when marriage has fallen into disrepute, as with the seven-year-old girl who had just seen the movie *Cinderella* and was testing her neighbor lady's knowledge of the story. The neighbor, anxious to impress the little girl, said, "I know what happens at the end." "What?" asked the girl. "Cinderella and the prince live happily ever after." To which the little girl answered, "Oh no, they didn't. They got married!" It was totally innocent, unwitting cynicism. But others are more calculated, like the famous literary figure William Congreve who wrote, "Every man plays the fool once in his life, but to marry is playing the fool all of one's life."[1]

FULLNESS IN MARRIAGE (vv. 18, 19)

These Scriptures are *radically elevating*. "Wives, submit to your husbands, as is fitting in the Lord. Husbands, love your wives and do not be harsh with them." This contrasts with the plight of women in the ancient world. William Barclay writes:

> Under Jewish law a woman was a thing; she was the possession of her husband, just as much as his house or his flocks or his material goods were. She had no legal right whatever. For instance, under Jewish law, a husband could divorce his wife for any cause, while a wife had no rights whatever in the initiation of divorce. In Greek society a respectable woman lived a life of entire seclusion. She never appeared on the streets alone, not even to go marketing. She lived in the women's apartments and did not join her menfolk even for meals. From her there was demanded a complete servitude and chastity; but her husband could go out as much as he chose, and could enter into as many relationships outside marriage as he liked and incur no stigma. Both under Jewish and under Greek laws and custom, all the privileges belonged to the husband, and all the duties to the wife.[2]

The domestic rules given here in Colossians were vastly different from those of the day. Wives here were addressed *equally* with their husbands, something radically new. Also, both husbands and wives had duties — not just the wives.[3] They were both admonished "in the Lord." The context of this phrase begins in verse 17, which makes it clear that the totality of their lives was to be regulated by it. This brought a vast dignity to both men and women.[4] They were both under the Lordship of Christ as equals. All of this was immensely elevating to women and would raise their positions greatly in the ancient and modern world.

At the same time, within the marital relationship these words established a definite *hierarchy*. As F. F. Bruce says, Paul "does hold that there is a divine instituted hierarchy in the order of creation, and in this order the place of the wife comes next after her husband."[5] However, this does not suggest (here or anywhere else in Scripture) that the wife is naturally or spiritually inferior to the husband, or vice versa. There is a hierarchy in the Holy Trinity, and yet equality. Orthodoxy teaches that the Son is simultaneously *equal* to the Father and *submissive* to him. Likewise, *equality* and *submissiveness* can coexist in human relationships, including the marriage relationship.

FULLNESS THROUGH THE WIFE (v. 18)

Christ's word to the woman in the Christian home is: "Wives, submit to your husbands, as is fitting in the Lord." I know of few statements that will rouse the ire of our modern assertive, rights-seeking, power-seeking culture than this. But it is God's Word, and we must resist those who would explain it away. It is God's design for fullness. Are there qualifications? Of course. "Submit" is not a synonym for servile, menial bondage. The appeal is to free responsible people and can only be heeded voluntarily. Moreover, none are called to follow it into sin or irrationality or harm of any kind. "We must obey God rather than men" (Acts 5:29). This is a charge for *Christians* who are living as *Christians*.

FULLNESS THROUGH THE HUSBAND (v. 19)

Verse 19 gives us the counterpart injunction: "Husbands, love your wives and do not be harsh with them." Here the commandment to men is just as radical as that to women. As Eduard Lohse has shown, such a command does not appear in any of the extra-Biblical household rules of the day.[6] The novelty of such a religious command must have struck the Colossian Christians with great power. Husbands were commanded to love their wives! What a novel thought! The command was not to *erotic* love (as some would expect) or to *friendship* love, but to *agape* love, which involves unceasing care and loving service for the wife's entire well-being. The Christian ethic for a husband's love for his wife was light-years beyond the formal domestic ethics of the day.

A parallel passage (Ephesians 5:25-33) gives the archetype of the love that is called for here, especially verse 25: "Husbands, love your wives, just as Christ loved the church and gave himself up for her." Thus, this radical command to love is only fulfilled when a husband loves his wife in imitation of Christ's love.

A husband's love must first, then, be *incarnational*. Genesis 2:24 anticipated this high call when it said, "a man will leave his father and mother and be united to his wife, and they will become one flesh." The idea is something of a *mutual* incarnation. With this ancient truth in mind Paul wrote in Ephesians 5:28, 29, "In this same way, husbands ought to love their wives as their own bodies. He who loves his wife loves himself.

After all, no one ever hated his own body, but he feeds and cares for it." This is a high call and may seem impossible. But it is possible to incarnate ourselves into our wives' *emotions* and *mental processes*. It is possible to have *spiritual* incarnation with her. It is possible to love our wives as we love our own bodies.

Dr. Robert Seizer, in his book *Mortal Lessons: Notes in the Art of Surgery*, tells of performing surgery to remove a tumor in which it was necessary to sever a facial nerve, leaving a young woman's mouth permanently twisted in palsy. In Dr. Seizer's own words:

> Her young husband is in the room. He stands on the opposite side of the bed, and together they seem to dwell in the evening lamp light, isolated from me, private. Who are they, I ask myself, he and this wry-mouth I have made, who gaze at and touch each other so generously, greedily? The young woman speaks. "Will my mouth always be like this?" she asks. "Yes," I say, "it will. It is because the nerve was cut." She nods, and is silent. But the young man smiles. "I like it," he says. "It is kind of cute." All at once I know who he is. I understand, and I lower my gaze. One is not bold in an encounter with a god. Unmindful, he bends to kiss her crooked mouth, and I, so close, can see how he twists his own lips to accommodate to hers, to show her that their kiss still works.[7]

It is possible to love your spouse as your own body. Practically, this means that the husband must do all he can to understand her world.

When my wife visited her sister in Connecticut, I was in charge of our four small children for a week. I fixed all the meals, changed thousands of diapers, fixed hurts, settled quarrels, gave baths, cleaned up catastrophes, and cleaned them up again. I was at work *before* I got up and *after* I went to bed. The experience so marked me that I invented a new kitchen, modeled on a carwash. The walls are tiles, and the floors slope to a large drain in the middle of the room. A hose hangs on the wall, nozzle ready to spray things down after the meal!

Loving incarnationally means we must work at spending *time* together. The June 1986 issue of *Psychology Today* carried an article entitled "Marriages Made to Last" in which they surveyed several hundred happily married couples. The interviews were conducted privately with each spouse alone. The top two things they said kept a marriage going were:

"My spouse is my best friend."

"I like my spouse as a person."

The researchers said good marriages develop among those who purposely spend a lot of time together.

Along with this, loving incarnationally means *listening*. As Howard Hendricks says, "Marriage is sometimes the dialogue of the deaf." The *Harvard Business Review* says 65 percent of an executive's time should be spent listening. So much more so in our most intimate relationships. "He who answers before listening—that is his folly and his shame" (Proverbs 18:13). Incarnational love spends time, listens, gives itself. Such is Christ's love.

Christ's archetypal love was not only *incarnational*—it was *sacrificial*, for he died for us. If we are to have a love like Christ's, we will be willing to die for our wives. This also calls us to a daily dying, and that is far more difficult. The rubber meets the road when we have to make a decision between free tickets to the baseball game and fixing the leaky faucets we promised to fix.

The positive side of dying is that we learn to live not only for Christ, but for our wives. When Anne Morrow married Charles Lindbergh, she was a timid, young woman, and he, having been the first to cross the Atlantic solo by air, was one of the most famous men in all the world. He *was* the American Eagle—a *bona fide* national hero. She could easily have been swept aside in all the adulation which came his way. But, loved by him, she grew to become one of our country's most popular writers. Here is how she puts it:

> To be deeply in love is, of course, a great liberating force and the most common experience that frees. . . . Ideally, both members of a couple in love free each other to new and different worlds. I was no exception to the general rule. The sheer fact of finding myself loved was unbelievable and changed my world, my feelings about life and myself. I was given confidence, strength, and almost a new character. The man I was to marry believed in me and what I could do, and consequently I found I could do more than I realized."[8]

The Eagle's soaring love caused shy delicate Anne Morrow Lindbergh to fly too. This is what sacrificial love can do. Sacrificial love mutually elevates both partners in the marital relationship.

Loving our wives as Christ loved the Church also involves *intercessory prayer*. Christ so perfectly participates in our lives that he perfectly prays for us. We husbands should strive to pray with the deepest "incarnational" knowledge possible. But we will be weak intercessors if we have failed to love our wives with incarnational sympathy. Peter says,

"Husbands, in the same way be considerate as you live with your wives, and treat them with respect as the weaker partner and as heirs with you of the gracious gift of life, so that nothing will hinder your prayers" (1 Peter 3:7). A foundering prayer life may be due to a failing in our most fundamental personal relationship. We must pray for our spouses in intimate detail, not just with a blanket beatitude. We must praise God for her strengths and lay her needs before him. She needs detailed prayer for what she faces each day, for how she relates with the children, for her interaction with the neighbors, for her many duties, for her insecurities, for her challenges.

We have seen two radical calls. One call is to wives: *submission*. The other is to husbands: to *love* as Christ loves. These cannot be read in isolation; they go together. It is unthinkably absurd for a Christian husband to demand submission of his wife if he is not radically loving her; likewise, it is errant logic for a wife who is not submissive to demand such love.

These brief words give us the pattern for fullness in Christian marriage — full love, full commitment, full exchange, full blessing. Whether we are beginning or far along, let us have no other goal than having the best marriages possible!

16

The Christian Family (II)

He began his life with all the classic handicaps and disadvantages. His mother was a powerfully built, dominating woman who found it difficult to love anyone. She had been married three times, and her second husband divorced her because she beat him up regularly. The father of the child I'm describing [the writer is Dr. James Dobson] was her third husband; he died of a heart attack a few months before the child's birth. As a consequence the mother had to work long hours from his earliest childhood.

She gave him no affection, no love, no discipline, and no training during those early years. She even forbade him to call her at work. Other children had little to do with him, so he was alone most of the time. He was absolutely rejected from his earliest childhood. When he was thirteen years old a school psychologist commented that he probably didn't even know the meaning of the word *love*. During adolescence, the girls would have nothing to do with him and he fought with the boys.

Despite a high IQ, he failed academically, and finally dropped out during his third year of high school. He thought he might find acceptance in the Marine Corps; they reportedly built men, and he wanted to be one. But his problems went with him. The other Marines laughed at him and ridiculed him. He fought back, resisted authority, and was court-martialed and thrown out of the Marines with an undesirable discharge. So there he was — a young man in his early twenties, absolutely friendless. He was small and scrawny in stature. He had an adolescent squeak in his voice. He was balding. He had no talent, no skill, no sense of worthiness.

Once again he thought he could run from his problems, so he went to live in a foreign country. But he was rejected there also. While there he married a girl who had been an illegitimate child and brought her back to America with him. Soon she began to develop the same contempt for him that everyone else displayed. She bore him two children, but he never enjoyed the status and respect a father should have. His marriage continued to crumble. His wife demanded more and more things that he could not provide. Instead of being his ally against the bitter world, as he hoped, she became his most vicious opponent. She could outfight him, and she learned to bully him. On one occasion she locked him in the bathroom as punishment. Finally she forced him to leave.

He tried to make it on his own, but he was terribly lonely. After days of solitude, he went home and literally begged her to take him back. He surrendered all pride. Despite his meager salary, he brought her $78.00 as a gift, asking her to take it and spend it any way she wished. But she belittled his feeble attempts to supply the family's needs. She ridiculed his failure. At one point he fell on his knees and wept bitterly as the darkness of his private nightmare enveloped him.

Finally, in silence he pleaded no more. No one wanted him. No one had ever wanted him.

The next day he was a strangely different man. He arose, went to the garage, and took down a rifle he had hidden there. He carried it with him to his newly acquired job at a book storage building. And from a window on the third floor of that building, shortly after noon, November 22, 1963, he sent two shells crashing into the head of President John Fitzgerald Kennedy.

Lee Harvey Oswald, the rejected, unlovable failure, killed the man who, more than any other man on earth, embodied all the success, beauty, wealth, and family affection which he lacked. In firing that rifle, he utilized the *one* skill he had learned in his entire, miserable lifetime.[1]

Lee Harvey Oswald's story stands out from that of others because of the incredibly documented public infamy of the final days of his life. His miserable life experience is paralleled today by thousands upon thousands who have known the same or even greater lack of affection, discipline, and training because much of the American family experience is a relational desert.

This chapter's short text contains the bare outline of what brings fullness to parent/child relationships. Again, as we observed with wives, this teaching beautifully elevated the position of children in the culture of that day. Under a section of Roman law entitled *Patria Potestes*, "The Power of the Father," the father could do anything he wanted with his children. He could sell them, turn them into slaves, even take their lives. But here, as with husbands and wives, both children and parents were presented as under God. The dominating example was the loving Fatherhood of God.

The instructions were given to children first: "Children, obey your parents in everything, for this pleases the Lord" (v. 20), and second to parents: "Fathers, do not embitter your children, or they will become discouraged" (v. 21).

INSTRUCTIONS TO CHILDREN (v. 20)

The first thing we should realize here is that discipline is indispensable if we are to have Christ's fullness in the home. Unfortunately, this is not true of American households in general. In the recently published letters between Karl Barth, the famous German theologian, and his friend Carl Zuckmayer, the celebrated German writer, Zuckmayer wrote:

> If one has lived in America and seen in countless cases what injustice is done to children, one has enough of it. One sees too much that someone, hidden behind misunderstood psychoanalytical maxims, allows them to become little tyrants and ill-humored despots, despots whom adults crawl in front of for pure convenience, only to get peace; and one sees how this takes effect in the unfortunate adolescents when they, brought up without authority are confronted with the difficulties of life.[2]

These foreign observers see the situation as an injustice, not so much to adults, but to children!

In this, their views are in perfect accord with the Bible, especially the writer of Hebrews: "For what son is not disciplined by his father? If you are not disciplined (and everyone undergoes discipline), then you are illegitimate children and not true sons" (12:7, 8). An evidence of being a child of God is God's discipline. So it is with human fathers. The absence of discipline means fatherhood is not being practiced, and weak, inconsistent discipline shows a lack of love. Discipline is therefore a key to child-parent fullness!

It is interesting to note that many psychologists are finding more evidence that discipline is, indeed, the great ingredient for domestic fullness. Dr. Stanley Coopersmith, associate professor of psychology at the University of California, surveyed 1,738 normal middle-class boys and their families, beginning in the preadolescent period and following them through to young manhood. After determining the boys with the best self-esteem, he then compared their homes and childhood influences with those of the boys having a lower sense of self-esteem. He found three important characteristics which distinguished them:

1. The high-esteem children were clearly more loved and appreciated at home than were the low-esteem boys. The parental love was deep and genuine, not just an empty display of words. The boys knew they were the object of pride and interest, increasing their own sense of self-worth.

2. The high-esteem group came from homes where parents had been significantly more strict in their approach to discipline. By contrast, the parents of the low-esteem group had created insecurity and dependence by their permissiveness. Furthermore, the most successful and independent young men during the latter period of the study were found to have come from homes that demanded the strictest accountability and responsibility. And as could have been predicted, the family ties remained the strongest — not in the wishy-washy homes — but in the homes where discipline and self-control had been a way of life.

3. The homes of the high-esteem group were also characterized by democracy and openness. Once the boundaries for behavior were established, there was freedom for individual personalities to grow and develop. The boys could express themselves without fear of ridicule, and the overall atmosphere was marked by acceptance and emotional safety.[3]

Discipline and obedience are indispensable if we are to experience the fullness that God wants for us in our homes.

The command "obey" is significant for two reasons. First, it is a different word than that used in verse 18 where wives are told to "submit" to their husbands. The word there suggests a voluntary submission, a choice; here the command is more absolute. The other reason this word is significant is that it really consists of two words ("listen" and "under") and can be read literally, "listen under your parents," or "really listen to your parents and do it!" Common phrases in America today are: "Are you listening to me?" "Did you hear what I said?" "Do you ever listen?" "Now, listen to me!" Obedience begins with listening.

Implicit in this also is, not just hearing and doing, but doing it with the right attitude. Children are all too often like the proverbial little boy who was told by his teacher to sit in the corner. As he sat there he was thinking, "I'm sitting down on the outside, but I'm standing up on the inside." The Scriptures call for a heart obedience to parents.

You will note too that it says, "in everything." Are there any exceptions? Of course. "We must obey God rather than men" (Acts 5:29). We are never to go against our conscience or Scripture to obey anyone. Nor must we sin or do anything irrational or harmful to us or anyone else in carrying out parental obedience. The command is not a *carte blanche* for a cruel parent! But these cases aside, the Scripture before us says that obedience "pleases the Lord." The parallel passage in Ephesians 6:1-3 similarly says, "this is right," and then goes on to say, "'Honor your father and mother' — which is the first commandment with a promise — 'that it may go well with you and that you may enjoy long life on the earth.'" The terrible relationships of Lee Harvey Oswald's early life so marked his psyche that he was bound for trouble — and in fact a shortened life. I believe there are millions who suffer less dramatic workings of this syndrome.

The point is, we have here a simple and powerful command to *all* children to truly, from the heart, obey their parents. Neglect of this command brings great sorrow, if not now, then surely later in life. But if obeyed, it brings fullness.

INSTRUCTIONS TO PARENTS (v. 21)

The other half of the commandment is: "Fathers, do not embitter your children, or they will become discouraged."

During much of my college years, I worked for a store which had a large part of the trade of the rodeo cowboys in southern California. I learned there are at least two ways to break a horse. One is with the progressive use of a halter, bit, blanket, and saddle. Done correctly, this can produce a full-spirited, obedient horse. Another way is sometimes used with especially difficult horses. The method is simple. The wrangler simply takes a 2 x 4 and knocks the recalcitrant horse to its knees. A horse, it is said, can be tamed this way, but with great cost. You will have a spiritless animal, an animal that though "obedient" will never be what it could have been. There are children who are like this. Their spirits have been broken, they are "obedient," but something is missing. They have, to use Paul's words in verse 21, "[lost] heart" (NASB). They withdraw and keep it all inside. Or they rebel when they get big enough. The results are painful either way.

COLOSSIANS

Paul's advice to parents who want to avoid this trap is: "Fathers, do not embitter your children." Notice that the advice is primarily to "Fathers," the reason being that this would be more typically a father's sin.[4] The husband is naturally away from the children more than the mother and is thus less in touch with their feelings and more prone to false judgments and unwise direction. The specific sense of the Greek word is to irritate one's children either by nagging or deriding them — putting them down.[5] The parallel in Ephesians 6:4 says, "Fathers, do not exasperate your children" and has the same idea of irritating them through perpetual fault-finding.

Millions of children, even in Christian homes, experience a constant rain of criticism. John Newton, the great preacher and hymn-writer, who experienced such a wretched life before turning to Christ, said, "I know that my father loved me — but he did not seem to wish me to see it."[6] Parents, fathers, discipline is to be given, but so is encouragement. Obedience is to be nurtured by love and praise. We must never cause our children to "lose heart."

Another kind of father who exasperates a child is the one given to irritability or grouchiness. Most people maintain a placid veneer at work because they *have* to do so. But at home . . . Only the Lord knows how many children "lose heart" because their fathers have hard days. This reminds me of a cartoon in which the boss is grouchy to his employee, who in turn comes home and is irritable with the children. His son, in turn, kicks the dog. The dog runs down the street and bites the first person he sees — the boss! We parents must never let our pressures drive us into this unhappy cycle. The costs are too high!

Others exasperate their children with their harsh and overstrict rules. Contemporary culture is especially filled with deadly traps. The tragic deaths of the Celtics' Larry Bias and Cleveland's defensive back Don Rogers seem to point out the extremes. Because of this, the zealous Christian parent can be tempted to say no to virtually everything his child asks. Rather, the parent should be looking for opportunities to say yes to as many things as he or she can conscionably say yes to. Our reasons for saying no must be valid, such as safety, morality, or health. Overstrictness (not strictness!) sometimes clothes a lazy approach to raising children.

Another way this can happen is through a father's capricious inconsistency. The poor horse who has a rider who is constantly digging his heels into its side and pulling the reins at the same time learns that nothing is ever right. So it is with the child who receives conflicting messages. As parents we must work at consistency. Of course, this does not mean we never change our minds, but wise parents will prompt each other *privately*, inviting all the criticism and help possible in being consistent parents.

Finally, perhaps one of the most exasperating things a parent can do is keep their children at a distance. An oft-quoted survey says that fathers spend an average of thirty-seven seconds a day with their children. Few things could be more disheartening and resentment-building than to hear your life directed, as it were, from a shadowy figure from Mount Olympus who leaves before you go to school, returns after dinner, and hands down edicts of conduct after church at Sunday dinner. Perhaps the character is a bit overdrawn, but there is no substitute for spending time with your children — and when you are with them, really be with them.

Parents, especially fathers, if we want to have all the fullness in our primary family relationships which God would have for us, we must discipline our children. To refrain from discipline is an act of hatred toward our own — unloving indifference — cruel permissiveness. But at the same time, our discipline must be given with encouragement. We must be patient, not irritable. While strict, we must not be overstrict. We must look for ways to say yes as well as no. We must be consistent and stable in our direction. We must spend time with our own, listening and loving.

17

The Christian Family (III)

COLOSSIANS 3:22–4:1

As we have explored the theme of domestic fullness, we have seen how Christ brings this fullness to the relationship of husband and wife (vv. 18, 19) and to fathers and children (vv. 20, 21). Now we see how Christ extends his fullness to masters and slaves.

Paul's teaching here was accompanied by a great amount of tension, for several reasons. Primary was the amazingly vast extent of slavery and its dehumanizing nature. Ancient historians estimate that there were some 60,000,000 slaves in the Roman Empire, or about one-half the population. Because of this, work was considered below the dignity of the slave-owning Roman free man. Practically everything was done by slaves, even doctoring and teaching. Though there were some felicitous relationships between masters and slaves,[1] basically the lot of a slave was not very happy. Ancient tradition, dating back to Aristotle, classified slaves as things, living tools. The Roman Varro classified farm implements into three classes: the articulate, the inarticulate, and the mute — the articulate being slaves. A later Roman writer recommended a grim utilitarianism in buying a farm: toss out the old slaves to die, because they were broken tools. Some did just that.

Gaius, the Roman lawyer, said, "We may note that it is universally accepted that the master possesses the power of life and death over a slave." If a slave ran away, he was branded on the forehead with the letter F for *Fugitivus* and sometimes even put to death, with no trial.[2] The situation of slaves in general was not good, and for some it was terrible. Thus a melancholy blanketed the lives of millions in the ancient world. Christianity's preaching of the gospel with its explicit doctrine of equality raised the tension. Consider, for example, Paul's teaching in Galatians 3:28 — "There is neither Jew nor Greek, slave nor free, male nor female, for you are all one in Christ Jesus."

We can be sure that Paul's teaching in Colossians 3:22 — 4:1 was attended eagerly by both slaves and masters in Colosse. That, no doubt, is why it was far more extensive than the previous domestic instruction to husbands/wives and children/fathers.

The advice Paul gives here was ultimately revolutionary, because in time it brought the downfall of slavery as an institution. But it was also immediately revolutionary in that it brought fullness to the Christian's life, whether slave or master. In the ancient world this was a *domestic* fullness, because slavery was an intensely personal family matter. Today the application is largely *professional* as we are either masters or serve our masters.

Today the average worker still divides five or six days of his week into more or less equal periods of eight hours work, eight hours sleep, and eight hours "free time." Work is so important that our society normally defines people by *what* they do. In order for Christ to bring fullness to life, he must bring it to what we do for a living, whether slave or master, employer or employee.

A FULL LIFE FOR SERVANTS/EMPLOYEES (vv. 22-25)

> Slaves, obey your earthly masters in everything; and do it, not only when their eye is on you and to win their favor, but with sincerity of heart and reverence for the Lord. Whatever you do, work at it with all your heart, as working for the Lord, not for men. (vv. 22, 23)

Hearing these words without explanation, one could easily say, "Paul, whose side are you on?" Think of how these words must have sounded to the exploited servant! "Slaves, obey your earthly masters in everything." Of course, the apostle was not encouraging submission to immoral or hurtful commands, and yet "everything" is so encompassing. Slaves were very often asked to do unpleasant things. This was a tough command, especially when linked with the next phrase: "not only when their eye is on you and to win their favor." The Greek is literally, "eye service," work that is only done when the boss is looking. We all know what that is like. In gym class, when the coach is watching there are perfect pushups. But when he looks away . . . Eye service results in half-done jobs. The room is swept, but the dirt is brushed under the carpet. Work breaks extend until the boss returns.

This is not the way it is supposed to be. Rather, our service is to be "with sincerity of heart," "with all your heart." This high call makes no distinction between pleasant or unpleasant tasks, dull or challenging, menial or interesting. It simply states that everything must be done energetically, from the heart, whether the boss is present or not. I have known some who have gotten themselves in trouble with fellow-workers because, in respect to this principle, they worked hard and were honest about their hours. Some hard-working Christians have even lost their jobs due to the lies said about them by their peers. Yet, we must obey the Lord.

If this high call stood alone, it would be supremely impossible. But it is accompanied by an enabling rationale: it is for the Lord. "Whatever you do, work at it with all your heart, as working *for the Lord,* not for men, since you know that you will receive an inheritance *from the Lord* as a reward. *It is the Lord Christ you are serving*" (vv. 23, 24, emphasis mine). It is this reality which inspires the great work of Mother Teresa in Calcutta. Taking Matthew 25 seriously, she believes that when she and her Sisters of Charity are cleansing sores and touching the ill for Christ, they are doing it to Christ. The most menial tasks — washing floors, scrubbing pots and pans — are *for* the Lord. Mother Teresa believes and does the truth! However, Mother Theresa's example must not promote an over-romanticizing of this truth. Most of us in our daily work are not dressing the sores of lepers or tending the dying. Some of us work "nothing" jobs. Some shuffle meaningless mounds of paper. Some dig holes and fill them up. Some can see nothing noble in the tasks they perform. They are nevertheless serving God as they work. This truth transformed the lot of the Christian slave in the ancient world. His "nothing" tasks were actually noble when done for Christ. Because of this, Christian slaves invariably brought higher prices in the slave market.[3]

At the end of verse 22, the apostle adds that our work is to be done in "reverence for the Lord." The pagan slave served his master because he was bound by fear; the Christian slave served his master *better* because he feared God. Working hard at our tasks from the heart brings glory to God.

In verses 24 and 25 the writer further enlarged the rationale for the believers' work ethic by adding that the God we serve will reward us: " . . . since you know that you will receive an inheritance from the Lord as a reward. It is the Lord Christ you are serving. Anyone who does wrong will be repaid for his wrong, and there is no favoritism." The "reward" will be good or bad, depending upon performance. All believers, though under the ultimate forgiveness of Christ, will have their works judged. "For we must all appear before the judgment seat of Christ, that each one may receive what is due him for the things done while in the body, whether good or bad" (2 Corinthians 5:10). This can, of course, be good or bad news, depending upon how we live our Christian lives. But to the first-century Christian slave this was largely good news, because under Roman law a slave could inherit nothing.[4] Yet here he learned that he could receive "an inheritance . . . a reward." God rewards faithful workers. This ought to be an encouragement to us, whatever our lot in life. God pays us so well that when we get to Heaven we will wish we had served him even more.

In verses 22 to 25 we have Paul's teaching regarding the work of slaves (employees) in the Colossian church. How does this impact our work ethic?

First, we must not suppose that if we try to live up to the Biblical teaching regarding work, all will go well on the job. I learned this early in life (on my very first job). I was fourteen years old and got an after-school job working at a nursery watering plants, stocking, and waiting on customers. I was anxious to do my very best, and I did. I was always on time, I never stood around, I looked for extra things to do. But I just could not please my boss, though he was a good man. Finally there came a payday when he took me aside and said, "You are terminated." That can, of course, happen at any age, and even when you are doing your very best as unto the Lord.

Second, the apostle's teaching here is not a call to overwork or workaholism. Correct as the Biblical ethic is, capitalism was and is easily perverted to the worship of work in the nineteenth and twentieth centuries, providing theological guise for addiction to wealth, power, and the exploitation of workers. This has happened in self-consciously Christian societies such as England where children were abused and exploited to an unbelievable degree. Today the exploitation is more subtle, but just as deadly. The ironic evils of *self*-exploitation in obsessive work habits touch virtually every family.

A third aspect of our work ethic is that Christians ought to be the *best* workers. I once had an employer tell me that he had become skeptical about Christian employees because of his experience with two theological students who seemed to be always standing around talking about God during work hours. But what really did it was when the boss observed one go into the bathroom for twenty minutes. When the employee emerged, he said to his fellow-student, "I just had the most wonderful time. I read three chapters of John in the john!"

Christians ought to be the best in attitude, the best in dependability, and the best in integrity. All of us who are employed must be faithful, hard workers or we are sinning.

Last, we must realize that there is intrinsic nobility in work offered to God. Gerard Manley Hopkins put it this way:

Smiting on an anvil, sawing a beam, white-washing a wall, driving horses, sweeping, scouring, everything gives God some glory if being in His grace you do it as your duty. To go to Communion worthily gives God great glory, but to take food in thankfulness and temperance gives Him glory too. He is so great that all things give Him glory if you mean they should. So then, my brethren, live.[5]

Our lives will be full when we do our very best, "not only when their eye is on you and to win their favor, but with sincerity of heart and reverence for the Lord" (v. 22).

A FULL LIFE FOR MASTERS/EMPLOYERS (4:1)

Masters, provide your slaves with what is right and fair, because you know that you also have a Master in heaven.

Remember, under Roman law the slaves had no rights at all. So these words had a strange ring to non-Christians, and to the newly believing master. Also, given the social conditions of the times, this command may have been more difficult to carry out than what was asked of the slaves. The master who attempted to provide his slaves "with what is right and fair" ran a deep risk of ostracism from his fellow slave owners, much like Christians today, such as Michael Cassidy in South Africa, who are living a Biblical ethic amidst the persecution of right and left.

The guiding reality for the master/employer is that both he and his servant have the same Lord: "you know that you also have a Master in heaven." Some have thought that this was too general. But as Alexander Maclaren said, "If we try to live that commandment for twenty-four hours, it will probably not be its vagueness of which we complain."[6] Employers, if you truly realize that you must answer to God for the way you conduct yourself with your employees, you will care about what happens to them. You will be concerned that they are paid properly. You will be concerned about their illnesses, their spouses, their children, their education. Along with this, you may have more problems. In fact, this kind of caring attitude assures that you will. But you will also have the fullness of Christ.

Masters/slaves — employers/employees, one thing is for sure: disregard the apostle's advice and you will never know fullness in your domestic/professional life, no matter how well you succeed. Disregard his advice and something will always be missing.

Jesus, who is the fullness of the universe, wants us to be full in our marital relationships, our family relationships, and our professional relationships. Moreover, he desires that this fullness overflow to the world. Justin Martyr wrote in the second century:

> Our Lord urged us by patience and meekness to lead all from shame and the lusts of evil, and this we have to show in the case of many who have come in contact with us, who were overcome and changed from violent and tyrannical characters, either from having watched the constancy of their Christian neighbors, or from having observed the wonderful patience of Christian travelers when overcharged, or from doing business with Christians.[7]

As people "do business" with us, may our fullness become their fullness!

18

The Fullness in Communication

COLOSSIANS 4:2-6

F or me, one of the most beautiful phrases in all of Scripture is the Apostle John's identification of Jesus as the "Word": "In the beginning was the Word" (John 1:1). Before the creation of all things, Christ was eternally continuing as the Word. As the "Word," Jesus is the ultimate communication of God. Before there was time or earth or water or fire, before we were, God had determined to communicate with us. "In the beginning was the Communication." John further writes, "The Word [the Communication] became flesh and lived for a while among us" (John 1:14). When Christ did this, he became to us the ABC of God, the alphabet of Deity. "We have seen his glory, the glory of the one and only Son, who came from the Father, full of grace and truth" (John 1:14). Because he is the Word, we understand something of how much we have always been loved. He spelled out God's love for us (John 3:16)!

This chapter's text calls us to fullness in communication with God, and to fullness in communicating with the world. Since Christ is the fullness of the universe and we have been made partakers of his fullness, our fullness should flow back up to him and out to the world.

FULLNESS IN COMMUNICATION WITH GOD (v. 2)

Devote yourselves to prayer, being watchful and thankful.

At the very heart of our communication must be full devotion to prayer. The idea here is persistence in prayer—continual prayer. Elsewhere the Lord himself encouraged this by telling the story of a widow who got her way with a godless, uncaring judge because she nagged him. It was "a parable," Luke says, "to show them that they should always pray and not give up" (Luke 18:1). Such continual prayer was the abiding experience of the Apostolic Church (Acts 1:14; 2:42). The apostles were constantly encouraging this, as did Paul when he challenged the Thessalonians to "pray continually" (1 Thessalonians 5:17)—full, continual communication with God.

How is this possible? Are we always to be carrying on a constant verbal dialogue, whatever we are doing? They have places for people who do this, and the doors lock from the outside! There cannot be unbroken verbal communication with God, otherwise we would never be really "there" for anything we did. But in another sense prayer is not so much the speaking of words as the posture of the heart.

The Quaker Thomas Kelly said in his *Testament of Devotion*:

There is a way of ordering our mental life on more than one level at once. On one level we can be thinking, discussing, seeing, calculating, meeting all the demands of external affairs. But deep within, behind the scenes, at a profounder level, we may also be in prayer and adoration, song and worship, and a gentle receptiveness to divine breathings.[1]

The delightful medieval monk Brother Lawrence wrote in the classic *The Practice of the Presence of God*:

The time of business does not differ with me from the time of prayer; and in the noise and clatter of my kitchen, while several persons are at the same time calling for different things, I possess God in as great tranquility as if I were on my knees.[2]

Full devotion to prayer is possible in a busy life. "Devote yourselves to prayer."

Paul continued, "being watchful and thankful." Being devoted to prayer does not mean the mind goes into a devotional neutral while an easy "stream of consciousness" flows between us and God. Rather, a habit of prayer demands mental alertness to the dangers of life and the needs of those around us, an awareness which can at any moment launch us into fervent prayer. Paul's parallel challenge in Ephesians 6:18 presents the attitude in no uncertain terms: "And pray in the Spirit on all occasions with all kinds of prayers and requests. With this in mind, be alert and always keep on praying for all the saints."

All of this is part of full communication with God. This devotion is vigilant, and is also wonderfully positive because it is "thankful." It remembers God's goodness. Joshua returned to Gilgal to gaze on the stones of remembrance (the stones taken from the Jordan when God held back the waters so Israel could cross). Thus he was refreshed, and his heart rejoiced in thanksgiving (Joshua 4). Likewise, we are to recall our stones of remembrance and give thanks in our communication with God.

Is your communication with God full? If not, it is because you are not appropriating his fullness (see 2:9, 10). If your life falls short, dip your cup in now. When your heart is overflowing, it will flow up to God in communication — alert and with an attitude of thanksgiving.

FULLNESS IN COMMUNICATION WITH THE WORLD (vv. 3-6)

Paul asked first for fullness in his own communication with the world: "And pray for us, too, that God may open a door for our message, so that we may proclaim the mystery of Christ, for which I am in chains. Pray that I may proclaim it clearly, as I should" (vv. 3, 4). Paul did not seem to care whether he was in prison or not — he just wanted more opportunity to communicate the Good News. It was preaching that got him into prison and would keep him in prison, and that was okay if he could preach more — and we know that he did! Paul burned to communicate the gospel. In 1 Corinthians 16:8, 9 we see him saying of his Ephesian ministry, "But I will stay on at Ephesus until Pentecost, because a great door for effective work has opened to me, and there are many who oppose me." When he left the Ephesian church, he told its elders that night and day for three years he had continuously admonished each one with tears (Acts 20:31). Paul's desire for opportunities to preach the mystery of Christ is a model for us.

In addition, Paul wanted to proclaim Christ's gospel "clearly" (v. 4). Unfortunately, this is not always the concern of preachers, as we often hear of "a mist in the pulpit and a fog in the pew." R. C. Sproul says, "I use big words to disguise my ignorance. Big words are great for that. If I can use a word that nobody understands, chances are people will think that at least I understand what I am talking about even if they don't."[3]

C. S. Lewis agrees: "Any fool can write *learned* language. The vernacular is the real test. If you can't turn your faith into it, then you either don't understand it or you don't believe it."[4]

Spurgeon once commented, "Christ said, 'Feed my sheep. . . . Feed My lambs.' Some preachers, however, put the food so high that neither sheep nor lambs can reach it. They seem to have read the text, 'Feed my giraffes.'"[5]

Joe Bayly, in his book *I Love to Tell the Story*, commented:

> Someone passed the following quotation on to me, from a graffiti wall at St. John's University in Minnesota: "Jesus said to them, 'Who do you say that I am?' And they replied, 'You are the eschatological manifestation of the ground of our being, the kerygma in which we find the ultimate meaning of our interpersonal relationships.' And Jesus said, 'What?'" I like that. I like it because it sets the simplicity of our Lord's words and teaching over against the complexity of some technical expressions of truth. Not that theology is wrong. We need deep thinkers who can explain the ramifications of our faith. But such complexity of ideas belongs in a seminary classroom, not on the hillside where Jesus taught multitudes, or in the room where I teach my Sunday school class. Jesus was profound, but simple in expression. To use an old but true way of expressing it, He put the cookies—or the bread of life—on the lowest shelf, where anyone could reach it. And so must I. I cannot show off my knowledge (the little that I have) or my vocabulary and still teach as Jesus taught. Nor get through to people as He got through to them.[6]

In saying to the Colossians, "Pray that I may proclaim it clearly, as I should," Paul acknowledged that prayer makes all the difference in communicating the gospel. There is a great story that comes from the life of Hudson Taylor. There was a mission station that was particularly blessed in the China Inland Mission, far above the others. There seemed to be no accounting for this, because others were equal in devotion and in ability. Hudson Taylor was traveling and speaking in England, and after a meeting a man came up and began to ask him about that particular station. Then he began to ask many personal questions. It turned out that the man had been the college roommate of the missionary at that station many years earlier, and he had committed himself to daily praying for the work there. Hudson Taylor said, "Then I knew the answer."

In verses 5 and 6 Paul expressed his concern for the Colossians' witness: "Be wise in the way you act toward outsiders; make the most of every opportunity. Let your conversation be always full of grace, seasoned with salt, so that you may know how to answer everyone." "Grace" in their speech presupposed grace in their hearts, "for out of the overflow of the heart the mouth speaks" (Matthew 12:34). As grace flows through the heart, it flows outward in kindness. This conversation is never insipid or boring. In fact, it is "seasoned with salt" — salty, savory, scintillating — not the dull, sanctimonious vocabulary that seems to be demanded in some church circles. It is thoughtful speech, words with content. It is joyful, even witty, for this is what salty speech meant in classical Greek.

Spurgeon, one of the greatest gospel communicators who ever lived, was once criticized by a woman who thought he was too witty. Spurgeon replied, "Madam, if you knew what I *didn't* say, you wouldn't say that!"

Believers and their gospel are to be interesting. Their remarks are to be contextualized; that is, they are to speak to the people where they are, according to their interests and needs. Becky Pippert, whose husband served as UPI Bureau Chief in the Middle East, wrote:

> Recently at a party I was introduced by a very staid diplomat with: "This is Becky and she really believes. She's really devout and she's so interesting!" Wes and I have laughed many times over how people have introduced us here with great enthusiasm, fascination and respect. This comes out of the context of our efforts to genuinely get to know these people and their interests. We go to concerts together, see films together and out of scores of conversations, our Christian beliefs have emerged. We don't do this as a gimmick to slip in the gospel. We do it because we are genuinely interested in relating to non-believers and their world views.[7]

This is full communication — speech filled with grace and salt, meeting the other person where he or she is. Let us "make the most of every opportunity" (v. 5).

Jesus Christ was and still is the Word. As such he is the ultimate communication to us. Our best response is to allow our hearts to overflow in communication.

Our hearts must flow back to God in continual, prayerful devotion, vigilance, and thanksgiving. They must flood the world with the gospel in clarity, grace, and salt.

This is proper communication for hearts filled with the fullness of God.

19

The Fullness
in Fellowship (I)
(Fully Transformed Lives)

COLOSSIANS 4:7-9

Myra Brooks Welch tells the story
of a battered, scarred violin held up for bid by an auctioneer who hardly
thought it worth his time. And it apparently wasn't, for the final bid was a
grudging three dollars. But as he was calling, "Three dollars once, three
dollars twice, going for three," a gray-haired man came forward and
picked up the bow, wiped the dust from the old instrument, tightened the
strings, and played the most beautiful melody — "as sweet as an angel
sings." When the music ceased, the auctioneer, holding it up with the
bow, said in a different tone, "What am I bid for the old violin?" Instead
of three dollars, it went for three thousand!

> The people cheered, but some of them cried,
> "We do not quite understand —
> What changed its worth?" The man replied,
> "THE TOUCH OF THE MASTER'S HAND."
> And many a man with a life out of tune,
> And battered and torn with sin,
> Is auctioned cheap to the thoughtless crowd.
> Much like the old violin.

A "mess of pottage," a glass of wine,
 A game and he travels on.
He's going once and going twice,
 He's going — and almost gone.
But the MASTER comes, and the foolish crowd
 Never can quite understand
The worth of a soul, and the change that's wrought
 By the TOUCH OF THE MASTER'S HAND.

Such change is incomprehensible for those outside. But all who have experienced that touch *perfectly* understand.

Some who have experienced the Master's touch are mentioned by name in the closing paragraphs of Paul's letter. The study of these ancient lives can bring a transforming touch to our modern lives and thus fullness in everyday service.

TYCHICUS: FULL SERVICE (vv. 7, 8)

The first name Paul mentioned was Tychicus, in verses 7 and 8: "Tychicus will tell you all the news about me. He is a dear brother, a faithful minister and fellow servant in the Lord. I am sending him to you for the express purpose that you may know about our circumstances and that he may encourage your hearts."

The Scriptures mention Tychicus only five times (here, Acts 20:4, Ephesians 6:21, 2 Timothy 4:12, and Titus 3:12), but we can draw some distinct conclusions about his experience and place in life. Tychicus popped up at the end of Paul's missionary work in Ephesus, and since he was a native of the province of Asia (Acts 20:4), of which Ephesus was the major city, we think he was probably a convert of Paul's long ministry in Ephesus. Very likely he had been born in that city, lived there, and found new life under Paul's ministry. Thus, he probably witnessed the great Ephesian silversmiths' riot against Paul, which prompted the apostle to leave Ephesus for Macedonia (Acts 19:35 – 20:1). As such Tychicus experienced danger himself and shared Paul's immense bravery. A short time later when Paul decided to return to Jerusalem, where he would ultimately be arrested, Tychicus was one of the seven who accompanied him as a traveling companion (Acts 20:4). Very likely he carried with him the Ephesians' offering for the poor in Jerusalem.

When Paul was arrested, Tychicus, along with Dr. Luke and others, stayed with Paul through the "thick and thin" of his arrest and imprisonment in Caesarea, his dramatic appearances before kings and governors, his miserable voyage and shipwreck en route to Rome, and his residence in Rome awaiting trial. Thus we see that Tychicus was a man of intense devotion to God and Paul. Paul said, ". . . I was shipwrecked, I spent a night and a day in the open sea, I have been constantly on the move. I have been in danger from rivers, in danger from bandits, in danger from my own countrymen, in danger from Gentiles; in danger in the city, in danger in the country, in danger at sea; and in danger from false brothers. I have labored and toiled and have often gone without sleep; I have known hunger and thirst and have often gone without food; I have been cold and naked" (2 Corinthians 11:25-27). Tychicus could have written this about himself as well, due to his remarkable loyalty to the apostle

Because of this, Paul chose him to travel as his messenger back to the churches of provincial Asia. As such, Tychicus was charged with two duties. First, to deliver Paul's letters: one to the Colossians, another to a slave owner in Colosse named Philemon, another to the Ephesians (see Ephesians 6:21), and quite probably a last letter to the Laodiceans (see Colossians 4:16). His second duty was simply to tell the churches in Asia about Paul's situation. Tychicus was Paul's errand boy! Later references in Titus 3:12 and 2 Timothy 4:12 confirm that he performed this humble function throughout Paul's life and ministry. Tychicus left no writings which survived. He did no feats which were thought worth preserving by Dr. Luke in Acts. He was a very common violin. However, God used him as a part of his divine symphony, and the music was beautiful.

Notice what our verses reveal about his character. In verse 7 Paul called him "a dear brother." He was greatly loved by Paul and the church in Rome, which is no small thing. Many kings and presidents and senators never accomplish this in life.

He was also called "a faithful minister" (or servant). There is no hint of his being a great thinker or orator, but only a *servant*, a title assumed by the Lord himself. Someone has said, "The greatest ability in the world is dependability," and, in this Tychicus was an immensely gifted man.

Paul rounded off his description with "fellow servant in the Lord." This term expressed an equality between Paul and Tychicus. It is almost as if Paul said, "Don't think because I wrote the letter and Tychicus is delivering it that I am better than he. We are both servants of the same Lord, who has given us separate tasks. I'm not Tychicus's master, though he is serving me."

From the beautiful teamwork of Paul and Tychicus we learn some great truths about fullness in service. *There is greatness in the smallest things done for Christ.* What would be the use of Paul's writing a letter if it did not get delivered? What would be the use of his towering thought in the opening chapters of Colossians and its compelling application if no one ever read it? "For the loss of a nail, lose a horseshoe; for the loss of a horseshoe, lose a horse; for the loss of a horse, lose a soldier; for the loss of a soldier, lose a battle; for the loss of a battle, lose a kingdom." What was the name of Charles Lindbergh's mechanic? Who blocked for O. J. Simpson when he won the Heisman Trophy? So it is with the seemingly small, unromantic things we do for Christ. Some of them are absolutely indispensable to God's work, and we will never know how much so until we get to Heaven.

When Tychicus was doing the smallest thing, he was serving Christ. We moderns run the danger of dichotomizing our lives into religious/non-religious, sacred/secular, great/small. But our Lord said and did otherwise: "I always do what pleases him" (John 8:29). Jesus, living in a human body for thirty-three years, never once performed a nonsacred act. God is in all our little deeds, and we ought to ask him to keep reminding us that it is so. We need to pray for this in our regular prayer times as well as in a thousand brief sighs.[1] How liberated our lives will then be.

We must realize that momentary things done for Christ are eternal. The letters which Tychicus bore to Asia would outlast the Roman Empire! Tychicus's name would be known until the end of time. The world may not see our part (rarely does it), but God does, and God says, "I will never forget their works."

The Colossian church now seems a failure. Today if you travel to the Lycus Valley, you will find only a few stones and some poor farmers. But in that day the church flourished, and its life spread contagiously around the world with the blessed truths of the supremacy of Christ. The Church now is far richer because of Colosse and Paul and his fellow servant Tychicus.

The life of this common, not remarkably gifted man who loyally served Christ and Paul graces all of our lives today. We know of Tychicus, but there are thousands who have equally blessed us whom we will only know in glory — common violins with whom the Master has made eternal music.

ONESIMUS: FULL TRANSFORMATION (v. 9)

Paul described another of the Master's servants in verse 9 as "Onesimus, our faithful and dear brother, who is one of you."

We know from Paul's letter to Philemon that Onesimus was Philemon's errant slave. From it we understand that Onesimus must have been a very difficult person, for Philemon had become a Christian and thus was not the overbearing, insensitive master that some were. His Christian theology taught that he and Onesimus were equal before God and would have to answer to God for their actions. Moreover, Onesimus as an unbelieving slave was, to quote his own self-evaluation, "useless" (Philemon 11). Miserable, ungrateful Onesimus had stolen from Philemon and fled to Ephesus and then on to Rome to become lost in the anonymity of the huge faceless populace — where instead of losing himself, he was found by his master's Lord, Jesus Christ.

An amazing transformation had taken place. Once restless and insolent, Onesimus was now clear-eyed and straightforward. Once ungrateful and unloving, Onesimus now abounded with love. Once dishonest, he was willing to make restitution. Once morose, he now entered joyfully into the psalms and hymns and spiritual songs of the persecuted church in Rome. Onesimus had been revolutionized by God's grace! Anytime a man or a woman voluntarily takes steps toward restitution, we can be sure something radical has happened. Some time ago I saw a newspaper clipping which had appeared in the *The East African Standard* in Nairobi:

ALL DEBTS TO BE PAID
I ALLAN HARANGUI ALIAS WANIEK HARANGUI, of P.O. Box 40380, Nairobi, have dedicated services to the Lord Jesus Christ. I must put right all my wrongs. If I owe you any debt or damage personally or any of the companies I have been director or partner i.e.
GUARANTEED SERVICES LTD.
WATERPUMPS ELECTRICAL
AND GENERAL CO. SALES AND SERVICE LTD.
Please contact me or my advocates J. K. Kibicho and Company, Advocates, P.O. Box 73137, Nairobi, for a settlement. No amount will be disputed.
GOD AND HIS SON JESUS CHRIST BE GLORIFIED

Here is a man with the spirit of Onesimus — so converted that it even touched his wallet. Christ does that! Recently in Nevada a man won $130,000 in a preliminary round of the poker world championship. Then he came to Christ and gave back $127,000 to get out of the final tournament. God's transforming grace is the same, whether in Rome or Las Vegas.[2]

God is still in the life-changing business today. I have seen him take a clever, filthy-mouthed young man and turn him into a masterful Christian executive who lives for Christ, his wife, and his family. I have seen a young woman who went for everything the self-worshiping culture of the seventies offered find Christ. Overnight she was elevated beyond her egoism, becoming a bright advertisement for Jesus. I have seen Christ take a young man lost in a middle-class desert of materialism and success — empty and rich — and fill him to overflowing. How does this occur? "For in Christ all the fullness of the Deity lives in bodily form, and you have been given fullness in Christ" (2:9, 10). Their emptiness became an opportunity for his fullness, their weakness for his strength, their thirst for his filling, their misery for his joy, their meaninglessness for his purpose.

> *A man with a life out of tune*
> *And battered and torn with sin,*
> *Is auctioned cheap to the thoughtless crowd,*
> *Much like the old violin.*

> *But the MASTER comes, and the foolish crowd*
> *Never can quite understand*
> *The worth of a soul, and the change that's wrought*
> *By the TOUCH OF THE MASTER'S HAND.*

Some may feel like their lives are "going once, going twice, going — almost gone." If so, what is needed is the touch of the Master's hand.

Edith Schaeffer tells the story of how the girl doing the cooking for L'Abri was supposed to be making the cakes, but made some errors until all she had left was an amorphous mess of goo. The logical thing was to throw it out. But the Schaeffers did not have extra money, and had learned to be very economical in the kitchen. So Mrs. Schaeffer sat down with the girl, figured out what was in the gooey mess, and by adding an extra ingredient was able to make what her husband described as "the most marvelous noodles you have tasted in your life." If we place ourselves in the Lord's hands, he can shape us into something which has both usefulness and beauty.[3]

Full transformation awaits those who invite the Master's touch. Full, overflowing service is the characteristic of life in Christ.

20

The Fullness
in Fellowship (II)

COLOSSIANS 4:10-14

When I came to Christ, I discovered an amazing new kinship with other believers, who were now my brothers and sisters by Biblical definition. My heart not only was drawn freely up to God, but ineluctably out to them. They loved the same things I loved. They wanted to talk about the same things I wanted to talk about. They understood. I was experiencing, of course, the fellowship, the Biblical *koinonia*, which every believer experiences as an outgrowth of knowing Christ.

My new life in Christ became the basis for lasting peer friendships. The shared mystery of Christ has been the basis for my relationship with my wife, Barbara, as well. In him our hearts beat together. She is not only my wife, but my best friend, my confidante, my counselor and joy.

In Christ we have developed mutual soul friendships with others which are among our dearest treasures. Indeed our regular prayers focus on them. Christian fellowship, and as a result friendship, is one of the principal boons of knowing Christ.

The dynamics of the Christian fellowship and friendship were beautifully explained by the Apostle John in 1 John 1:3 — "We proclaim to you what we have seen and heard, so that you also may have fellowship with us. And our fellowship is with the Father and with his Son, Jesus Christ." A primary motivation behind John's proclaiming of the gospel was that his hearers be brought into fellowship with the Father and Son, *and thus into fellowship with John and the Church*! Fellowship with the Godhead spawns fellowship with other believers.

The key to the quality of our earthly fellowship is the quality of our fellowship with God. Those with the richest fellowship with God have the richest fellowship with each other. They share the same view of *reality* as they regard the world around them. They share the same view of *self*, and understand the reality of sin as it affects the human personality. They share the same *values and ethical standards*. They share the same *love* for Christ, his Church, and his Word. They share the same *hopes* and the same *cause* — all of which makes for an exhilarating, satisfying mutuality.

That is why a businessman, Allan Emery, amidst the rush of the Thirtieth Street Station in Philadelphia, could hear the conductor whistling a refrain from a hymn, greet him in the Lord, and have an exchange of soul in a few brief moments that he will remember the rest of his life.[1] We have all experienced the same thing. Sometimes hardly a word is spoken, but there is an immediate sense of oneness and the ability to communicate on the deepest level. You sense that you both belong — that you are family.

In Colossian terminology, the fullness of Christ floods our souls and overflows to others. If the others are believers, their lives also overflow. There is mutual recognition and mutual refreshment in fellowship with believers. In the book of Acts there are more than 100 different Christians associated with Paul. He named sixteen different friends in Romans 16 alone![2] Here in Colossians he was true to form as he named ten people in closing. This, along with what we can cull from their backgrounds and from the nature of their greetings, suggests an overflowing fullness of fellowship in Christ.

FELLOWSHIP CROSSING RACIAL AND RELIGIOUS BARRIERS

In this passage six individuals sent greetings (through Paul) from Rome to Colosse. Three were Jews and three Gentiles. The three Jews (vv. 10, 11) were Aristarchus, Mark, and Jesus called Justus. Paul said of them, "These are the only Jews among my fellow workers for the kingdom of God, and they have proved a comfort to me." Then he went on to name the Gentiles: Epaphras, Luke, and Demas (vv. 12-14). Language, national animosities, and differences in religion and culture had divided the world of that day into hostile camps which could only be held together by the sword. Here under Paul's aegis both camps were meeting together willingly and lovingly — an amazing unity!

From the very beginning Jesus had demonstrated that this was the intent of the gospel. When he crossed forbidden barriers in reaching out to the Samaritan woman, as recorded in John 4, the woman was amazed, and the Jews who heard of it even more so. Hatred between Judea and

Samaria had lasted over 400 years. While the Jews had kept their racial purity during the Babylonian captivity, the Samaritans had lost theirs by intermarrying with the Assyrian invaders. To Jewish eyes this was unforgivable. Also, the Samaritans had built a rival temple on Mt. Gerizim — only to have it destroyed by the Jews in Maccabean times. In Christ's time bitter hatred reigned supreme. A Jewish prayer even included, ". . . and, Lord, do not remember the Samaritans in the Resurrection."

Added to this was the fact that the Samaritan was a "woman." (Strict rabbis forbade other rabbis to greet women in public. Some Pharisees were called "the bruised and bleeding Pharisees" because they shut their eyes whenever they saw a woman and so stumbled into the street, incurring pious bruises.) But Jesus not only spoke to the woman, he used the woman's drinking utensil, thereby becoming ceremonially defiled — a scandalous act. Jesus leapt far beyond the conventional barriers of his day! And in doing so, he modeled one of the supreme glories of the Church. Jesus not only reaches people like me, he does not just reach people like you, he does not reach just rich people, he does not only reach poor people, but all of us, and he brings us together.

This is what had happened in Rome (and elsewhere), but it had not been easy. The Gentiles in Rome were ready to mix, but it was not so with the Jewish believers who legalistically demanded that the Gentiles be circumcised and follow Jewish ceremonial law. When Paul came to Rome, these legalistic-minded Jewish believers gave him a cool reception, even rejecting the authenticity of his missionary charge. Only the three Jews named here helped him. They were receptive and loving; they understood grace; and so here they sent their greetings to the Colossian church. These three had the "Colossian fullness." It is impossible to hold racial prejudices in the heart and be Spirit-filled; such goes against everything Christ taught and teaches. When a Christian refuses fellowship with other healthy, Spirit-filled believers, there can only be one conclusion: something is wrong in his or her relationship to God. When we are having fullness of fellowship with the Father and his Son Jesus Christ, we have fellowship (and friendship!) with one another regardless of background. Three Jewish believers in Rome were experiencing fullness in fellowship, and it was overflowing to the church in Colosse.

FELLOWSHIP TRANSCENDING GRIEVANCES

Believers at their worst are capable of holding on to grievances. Two congregations, located only a few blocks from each other in a small community, thought it might be better if they would become one united body, and thus larger and more effective, rather than two struggling churches. But they were not able to pull it off. They could not agree on how to recite "The Lord's Prayer." One group wanted, "forgive us our trespasses," while the other demanded, "forgive us our debts." So one church went back to its *trespasses*, while the other returned to its *debts*! Believers can be stubborn, unchanging and unforgiving. But others, like Paul and Mark, are able to forgive and forget.

Earlier young Mark (John Mark) had accompanied Paul and Barnabas on Paul's first great missionary journey when they set out from Antioch. After ministering in Cypress, John Mark abandoned Paul when they reached the shores of Pamphylia, returning to Jerusalem. We do not know why. We can guess from Paul's writings that the hardships were incredible, with stress very much like that experienced by combat soldiers. Later, when Paul was planning another journey, Barnabas insisted that John Mark come along, and Paul refused. The result was the famous separation as Barnabas took John Mark with him and Paul recruited Silas. Paul was not running "Holy Land Tours," and he did not want anyone who had been fainthearted on his team. But now, twelve years later, John Mark was with Paul in Rome, ministering to him in his imprisonment. As Paul sent Mark's greeting to Colosse, he even commended him saying, "if he comes to you, welcome him" (v. 10). In the accompanying letter to Philemon he called him his "fellow worker" (Philemon 24). And later, at the sunset of his ministry, he said to Timothy, "Only Luke is with me. Get Mark and bring him with you, because he is helpful to me in my ministry" (2 Timothy 4:11).

There was no way that two men who both loved God and were walking in fellowship with him would not have fellowship with one another. This is what true fellowship brings! If two believers cannot be reconciled, then either both or one is not in fellowship with God. Is there someone that you will not forgive — that you have no desire to forgive though this person has humbly sought your forgiveness? If so, you need the fullness of Christ. If you are full of him, you will be like him — forgiving.

FELLOWSHIP WHICH IS LARGE-HEARTED

The expansiveness of Christian fellowship is seen in the desire of the six to send greetings to those in Colosse. Most of the six had never been to Colosse, but they loved the believers there anyway. They understood that they were all part of each other.

What Paul said about Epaphras suggests something of what they were like: "Epaphras, who is one of you and a servant of Christ Jesus, sends greetings. He is always wrestling in prayer for you, that you may stand firm in all the will of God, mature and fully assured. I vouch for him that he is working hard for you and for those at Laodicea and Hierapolis" (vv. 12, 13). Epaphras was from Colosse. He had come all the way to Rome because he was concerned about the Gnostic heresy which threatened to rob the Colossians of their fullness. Epaphras had a profound concern for his fellow-believers. Paul represented him as "always wrestling in prayer for you." From the Greek word used here we get our English word *agonize*. Paul had watched Epaphras pray for Colosse, and this was the one word which best described his prayer. The same root word was used to describe Jesus' fervent prayer in Gethsemane (Luke 22:44).

Epaphras cared! He prayed that they would "stand firm in all the will of God." His prayer was specifically directed against the heretics who falsely offered perfection and fullness through their system. The Colossians already had divine perfection in Christ. "God, help them to stay there!" prayed Epaphras. This was selfless, giving, big-hearted prayer.

Paul concluded his brief portrait of Epaphras by saying, "I bear him witness that he has a deep concern [literally, pain or distress] for you and for those who are in Laodicea and Hierapolis" (NASB). When you are in full fellowship with Christ, you naturally take on something of his heart for others, and this overflows in "deep concern." Phillips Brooks, the peerless preacher of Boston, put it this way:

> To be a true minister to men is always to accept new happiness and new distress. The man who gives himself to other men can never be a wholly sad man; but no more can he be a man of unclouded gladness. To him shall come with every deeper consecration a before untasted joy, but in the same cup shall be mixed a sorrow that it was beyond his power to feel before.[3]

That is the way it was with Epaphras and his coworkers. His enlarged heart made him vulnerable to the burdens of others.

Also, fullness in fellowship encompasses "marginal" people. Paul concluded the greetings with, "Our dear friend Luke, the doctor, and Demas send greetings" (v. 14). Luke was the only Gentile writer of any book in the New Testament. He was a much-loved Christian, physician, devoted friend, careful historian — all in one! But Demas is another story. Later Paul would write of him, "Demas, because he loved this world, has deserted me" (2 Timothy 4:10). Perhaps Paul was already aware of Demas's spiritual slide because he was the only one of the six about whom there was no comment in the greeting. Christian fellowship is not meant to be perfect. It must always be stretching.

Some draw a circle that shuts men out;
Race and position are what they flout;
But Christ in love seeks them all to win,
He draws a circle that takes them in!
(Edwin Markham, altered)

Our Lord even takes in those who disappoint and hurt. Christian fellowship makes us bigger people who have a greater capacity for sorrow — and for joy.

We have something wonderful to offer to the world: "We proclaim to you what we have seen and heard, so that you also may have fellowship with us. And our fellowship is with the Father and with his Son, Jesus Christ" (1 John 1:3). We offer first fellowship with God — not just knowledge of God, but a relationship with him. The gospel also offers a fullness of fellowship with his children. This dynamic fellowship:

- overcomes barriers.
- transcends grievances.
- produces largeness of heart.

Through believing in Christ, all can have this fullness of fellowship, for he offers it to everyone.

21

The Fullness of Paul's Heart

For those of us who claim the name of Christ, there are two distinct courses of life available. One is to cultivate a small heart. It is by far the safest way to go because it minimizes the sorrows of life. If our ambition is to avoid the troubles of life, the formula is simple: minimize entangling relationships, do not give yourself to people, carefully avoid elevated and noble ideals. If we will do this, we will escape a host of afflictions. Many people, even some who profess to be Christians, get through life with a minimum of tribulation by having small hearts.

The other path is to cultivate a ministering heart like that of the Apostle Paul. Open yourself to others and you will become susceptible to an index of sorrows scarcely imaginable to a shriveled heart. Enlarge your heart and you will enlarge your potential for pain.

The effects of these two kinds of hearts upon those around them are drastically different. Little hearts, though safe and protected, never contribute anything. No one benefits from their restricted sympathies and vision. On the other hand, large hearts, though vulnerable, also know the most joy and leave the greatest imprint on other hearts. Cultivate deafness and we will never hear discord, but neither will we hear the glorious strains of a great symphony. Cultivate blindness and we will be spared the ugly, but we will never see the beauty of a sunset or a bird on wing. Cultivate a small heart and life may be smooth sailing, but we will never know the heady wind of the Holy Spirit in our sails, the power and exhilaration of being borne along by the Spirit in accomplishing great eternal things for God. Cultivate a small heart, and we certainly will never have a great heart like the Apostle Paul's.

As we come to the final paragraph of the book of Colssians, we need to remind ourselves of the background of the book of Colossians. Paul was under house arrest in Rome, chained to a Praetorian guard night and day. His feet, which had trod the length of the Roman Empire, now could scarcely find room to pace. His eyes, which were always on the Gentile world, were now restricted to four walls. But his great heart, though caged in prison, would continue to mark the world as Paul wrote some of his most powerful letters, part of the Holy Scriptures.

Far away, over 1,000 miles distant, beat a similar heart in a man by the name of Epaphras, a leader in a tiny house church in Colosse. Epaphras had probably come to know Christ when Paul was ministering in Ephesus, and had gone back to the Lycus Valley where God used him to bring the Good News to its towns. People were coming to Christ regularly; the fruits of the Spirit were everywhere evident among the people.

It seemed to some that it would not be long until everyone in Colosse believed. But there were dark forces at work. Men and women began to attend their fellowship who brought with them an intimidating air of superiority. They explained that they liked what they saw in the church, for it was a promising beginning to a deeper, more fulfilling knowledge of God. So with conscious patience (the kind people use with inferiors) they explained that Christ could not be the Creator, and his incarnation at best was an illusion because God could not touch physical matter. The way to a true knowledge of God's fullness was by using ascetic disciplines and secret passwords to work one's way up a long series of emanations until they finally reached God. It was so intellectual and appealing, and some of the Colossians were led away from their fullness to the desolation of Gnosticism. Epaphras did his best against this heresy, but he needed help. And so, perhaps after some restless nights, he decided to seek Paul out in Rome.

No one knows by what port he entered Italy or how he found Paul in Rome, but we can surmise that their meeting was emotional and intense as Epaphras poured out his concern to the chained apostle. The effect on Paul was completely predictable, as it always is with enlarged hearts. Epaphras's concern became Paul's. A wonderful apostolic anxiety engulfed Paul's heart, as was common with him: "I face daily the pressure of my concern for all the churches. Who is weak, and I do not feel weak? Who is led into sin, and I do not inwardly burn?" said Paul to the Corinthian church (2 Corinthians 11:28, 29). To the Galatians he said, "I fear for you, that somehow I have wasted my efforts on you" (Galatians 4:11). Out of the same concern, Paul once sent a friend to the Thessalonians to find out about their faith, for fear that the Tempter might have tempted them and his labor be in vain (1 Thessalonians 3:5). Epaphras now had a soul brother in his concern!

Immediately Paul's brilliant, original intellect set itself to analyzing the Colossian problem: Here is a little church overflowing with the joy of new faith, and now comes a desolating philosophy which, ironically, is beguiling the people away from their fullness by promising a bogus fullness! Paul prayed and meditated much, and when his heart and mind were full, he called for his secretary and began to dictate. During the next hour, under the inspiration of the Holy Spirit, Paul gave the world the beautiful letter to the Colossians, a letter written to perpetuate the Colossians' fullness and ours.

We will review Paul's argument and then cap it off with his overflowing conclusions.

PAUL'S FULL-HEARTED ARGUMENT

Paul began, in the opening verses, with a celebration of the miracle of the tiny Colossian church in the Lycus Valley, a church which he had never seen. He especially celebrated the gospel, which had produced the remarkable faith, hope, and love of the new church.

Paul followed with a prayer for the Colossians' knowledge (1:9-14). The Gnostics had promoted their knowledge (*gnosis*) as the way to fullness. So Paul prays for the *epignosis* of Christ for the Colossians. Specifically, he prays for God "to fill you with the knowledge of his will through all spiritual wisdom and understanding . . . in order that you may live a life worthy of the Lord" (vv. 9, 10).

Having finished his prayer, he went on in verses 15 to 18 to give the most stupendously full revelation of Christ to be found in any of the epistles. It was a sublime poem/hymn of Christ's supremacy which speaks for itself:

> He is the image of the invisible God, the firstborn over all creation. For by him all things were created: things in heaven and on earth, visible and invisible, whether thrones or powers or rulers or authorities; all things were created by him and for him. He is before all things, and in him all things hold together. And he is the head of the body, the church; he is the beginning and the firstborn from among the dead, so that in everything he might have the supremacy.

According to this, Christ is supreme in four ways:

First, because he is "the firstborn over all creation" (v. 15), which in Hebrew thought means *first in rank or honor*. He is completely supreme in creation. There is none higher; there is no Gnostic god above him. One day every knee will bow to the name of Jesus, and every tongue will confess that Jesus Christ is Lord (Philippians 2:10, 11).

Second, he is supreme because he is Creator: "For by him all things were created: things in heaven and on earth, visible and invisible, whether thrones or powers or rulers or authorities; all things were created by him and for him" (v. 16). He created the invisible spirit world. He created the vast physical world. Einstein estimated that there are ten octillion stars in the universe. How many is that? Well, one thousand thousands make one million; 1,000 millions make one billion; 1,000 billions make one trillion; 1,000 trillions make one quadrillion; 1,000 quadrillions make one quintillion; 1,000 quintillions make one sextillion; 1,000 sextillions make one septillion; 1,000 septillions make one octillion. Ten octillion! − 10,000,000,000,000,000,000,000,000,000,000. Jesus created them all. He created the unseen microcosms, the incredible rainbow, the beauty of the cell, and he did it all *ex nihilo*, out of nothing. He did it by the word of his power!

Third, he is the sustainer of creation: "He is before all things, and in him all things hold together" (v. 17). The perfect tense here tells us that he continues to hold all things together, and that apart from his continuous activity all would disintegrate. He holds every speck of matter and every incorporeal spirit together. He is not contained in matter, but simply holds it together by his word! The Gnostics never dreamed of a God like this!

Fourth, he is the goal of creation: "all things were created by him and for [*towards*] him" (v. 16). All creation is moving toward its goal in him. All things sprang forth at his command, and all things will return to him at his command. He is the beginning and he is the end.

What we think of Christ is everything! If you believe that Christ is *eternal*, without beginning and without end, that he always was continuing; if you believe that he is *Creator* of everything, every cosmic speck across trillions of years of trackless space, the Creator of textures and shapes and colors which dazzle our eyes; if you believe that he is the *sustainer* of all creation, the force which is presently holding the universe together, and that without him all would dissolve; if you believe that he is the *goal* of everything, that all creation is moving toward him; if you believe this, nothing much can go wrong with you! We cannot think too highly of Christ.

This is the heart of the book of Colossians. Everything else flows from it, for this Christ is the One who "fills everything in every way"

(Ephesians 1:23). Christ's fullness makes full reconciliation possible, "For God was pleased to have all his fullness dwell in him, and through him to reconcile to himself all things . . . by making peace through his blood, shed on the cross" (vv.19, 20). Christ's fullness makes it possible for his blood to reconcile all who trust him and to effect the redemption of creation. His fullness makes the ministry of the gospel supreme (1:24-29). His fullness motivates Paul's supreme concern for the Colossians (2:1-5) and elicits a supreme charge to walk in Christ (2:6, 7).

Now Paul warned them not to fall captive to Gnostic foolishness, and then gave a rationale based on Jesus' fullness: "For in Christ all the fullness of the Deity lives in bodily form, and you have been given fullness in Christ" (2:9). Christ is full with all the fullness of Deity, and we, as Christians, are full of his fullness. It is incumbent upon us to have our lives open up more and more so we can receive this fullness — to cultivate an elasticity of soul. That is an antidote to dull, insipid Christianity.

In the remainder of Chapter 2, Paul explained more of the dynamics of this fullness (vv. 11-15), and successively warned them against Gnostic legalism, mysticism, and asceticism.

Colossians 3:1-4 bears the high point of exhortation in the letter:

> Since, then, you have been raised with Christ, set your hearts on things above, where Christ is seated at the right hand of God. Set your minds on things above, not on earthly things. For you died, and your life is now hidden with Christ in God. When Christ, who is your life, appears, then you also will appear with him in glory.

Our minds and hearts must consistently be focused upward. We cannot be too heavenly-minded! Sometimes we hear people say, "He is so heavenly minded, he's no earthly good." But they are wrong. He may be so self-righteous, so pious, so "goody-goody," but never too heavenly minded. This is, I believe, what made Paul stand above even the other apostles. He wrote, "I know a man in Christ who fourteen years ago was caught up to the third heaven. Whether it was in the body or out of the body I do not know — God knows. And I know that this man . . . was caught up to Paradise. He heard inexpressible things, things that man is not permitted to tell" (2 Corinthians 12:2-4). Paul was the man in this vision, but he humbly used the third person. This experience marked his life with the eternal, and it made him different.

As Joe Bayly expressed it, "Lord, burn eternity into my eyeballs." Only when it is thus can we really live! "Since, then, you have been raised with Christ, set your hearts on things above, where Christ is seated at the right hand of God. Set your minds on things above, not on earthly things. For you died, and your life is now hidden with Christ in God."

Paul followed this with marvelous practical exhortations regarding putting off the old man and putting on the new (3:5-14). In 3:15 — 4:1 he issued a series of challenges for church and family. His rationale was sublime: since Christ is the *cosmic* fullness, he is also the one who brings relational, *domestic* fullness to our lives. We ought to live in the fullness of his peace, his word, and his name (vv. 15-17). This cosmic fullness must bring domestic fullness to husband and wife (vv. 18, 19), parents and children (vv. 20, 21), and employers and employees (3:22 — 4:1). When we are all tuned to him, we are automatically tuned to each other. Because we receive direction from the same conductor, the music we play is in harmony.

Finally, this fullness brings fullness of communication with God in prayer and fullness of communication with the world (4:2-6).

Paul ended his letter by elaborating the fullness of fellowship with believers in a final greeting. Now we will take a brief look at those final greetings, Paul's personal salutation.

PAUL'S FULL-HEARTED CONCLUSION

Paul's final greeting was a three-part encouragement. First, in verse 15: "Give my greetings to the brothers at Laodicea, and to Nympha and the church in her house." Paul had never been to Laodicea either, but his large-heartedness compelled him to greet the church there and the woman, Nympha, who so graciously hosted it.

Second, in verse 16: "After this letter has been read to you, see that it is also read in the church of the Laodiceans and that you in turn read the letter from Laodicea." Paul encouraged an exchange of the letters he was sending to Laodicea and Colosse. He wanted them read aloud *as Scripture*.[1] We know that in the future Laodicea would need all the help it could get, as it became a church that was neither hot nor cold and was rejected by Christ (Revelation 3:14-22).

Third, in verse 17 he encouraged a young leader in the Colossian church: "Tell Archippus, 'See to it that you complete the work you have received in the Lord.'" From Philemon 2 many deduce that Archippus was the son of Philemon and Apphia. Perhaps Epaphras told the apostle of Archippus's budding spiritual life and potential. At any rate, Paul reminded him that his ministry originated "in the Lord." It was divinely given and must be treated as such. Paul told him that he must "complete" it, calling to mind for the final time the grand theme of fullness.

For perhaps an hour now Paul had been caught up in the sublime themes of Colossians. But now he stretched out his hand for the stylus to write his last words, and as he did so, the chain which fastened him to the Praetorian guard at his side hindered him. He reawoke to the consciousness of his prison. The exhaustion after such an hour of high communion made him consciously dependent, and all his profound teaching, all his thunderings and lightnings, ended in the simple cry which goes straight to the heart: "I, Paul, write this greeting in my own hand. Remember my chains. Grace be with you."[2] Paul was in jail, but no power on earth could cage his soaring heart. He had made himself vulnerable and thus knew deep miseries. But he also knew the winds of the Holy Spirit in his sails and he had been flying!

Paul closed with the apostolic benediction, "Grace be with you." A closing word of grace was the trademark of Paul in all his letters. "May God's unmerited, freely given favor rest on you." The communication of God's grace to a needy, sinful world is the end of God's deeds, and it is the end of this letter. John put it this way: "The Word became flesh and lived for a while among us. We have seen his glory, the glory of the one and only Son, who came from the Father, full of grace and truth. . . . From the fullness of his grace we have all received one blessing after another" (John 1:14, 16).

Have you received Christ's fullness? Say, "Here's my cup, Lord; fill it up, Lord." May we hold the miracle of being filled with the fullness of God high before us. May we seek those things that are above where Christ is seated at the right hand of God. There is more fullness for our lives as we open our lives more fully to him. May we experience that, and may the theme of this great epistle burn into our lives.

May we be filled to overflowing with Jesus Christ!

22

The Reconciling Wisdom

PHILEMON 1-25

It is difficult to say why Onesimus ran away from his master Philemon. Some say it was because Philemon was a harsh taskmaster. But that hardly seems likely from what the Scriptures reveal of that master's character. Far more probable is the supposition that Onesimus was a lazy, ungrateful servant with a dishonest streak who saw his chance to make off with a big chunk of his master's savings and did it, leaving Philemon deeply hurt and in financial straits. Though we do not know how Onesimus made his getaway, whether under the cover of darkness or in the guise of a business trip, the direction of flight was predictable — Rome. Maybe he fled to Ephesus where he purchased some handsome clothing which would identify him as a well-to-do man of the road; then he hopped a ship bound for Rome, disembarked at the Italian port of Puteoli, and made his way to Rome where, the historian Tacitus said, "all things horrible and disgraceful find their way."[1] There he melded into the dark sordid world of alias names, lawlessness, and immorality, and there he and his money were soon parted.

Onesimus was in big trouble, for he was guilty of *two* capital crimes: running away and theft. They were capital because they were sins against the existing social order. If allowed to spread, they would mean the demise of slavery and the Roman Empire, for the Empire was built on slavery. Rebellious slaves, if not eliminated, were at least branded on the forehead with F for *Fugitivus* (Fugitive) or CF for *Cave Furem* (Beware of thief!). Onesimus theoretically could have gotten both, if his master was in a *good* mood.

Almost contemporary to this letter to Philemon, Pedanius Secundus, a wealthy Roman, was murdered by one of his 400 slaves. During the

161

trial, Tacitus reports, the prosecution argued for the execution of all 400 slaves. The prosecution won, and the 400 were publicly executed as an example.[2] In the hands of a cruel master, Onesimus could have been subjected to a cruel death. Onesimus was in immense trouble. Slave hunters, with descriptions and warrants in hand, often mixed among the transient population of Rome.[3] It is very probable that Onesimus used a pseudonym and at times even disguised himself.

We do not know how he happened upon Paul. Perhaps he was down and out, heard Paul's name discussed, remembered his contact with Philemon, and sought him out for help. Whatever the case, he returned again and again and was truly converted! And his life was changed.

Mickey Cohen was one of the most infamous gangsters of the fifties, and something of a publicity hound. On one occasion he visited an evangelistic meeting and there showed an interest in Christ. Christian leaders, realizing that Cohen's conversion could have a great influence upon others, visited him regularly. One night after a lengthy conversation on Revelation 3:20, he "opened the door of his life." There were great expectations, but as the months passed there was no substantive change in the gangster's life. Finally his Christian friends confronted him. Cohen responded that "no one had told him he would have to give up his work or his friends. After all, there were Christian football players, Christian cowboys, Christian politicians; why not a Christian gangster?"[4]

Onesimus was not like that. Christ was *everything* to him, and he was totally transformed. Soon he became one of Paul's devoted disciples, doing whatever he could to ease his imprisonment — running errands, doing manual labor to help with expenses, counseling others. As Onesimus grew, the conviction that he must return to Philemon also grew. Perhaps he had heard of the Lord's words from the Sermon on the Mount: "Therefore, if you are offering your gift at the altar and there remember that your brother has something against you, leave your gift there in front of the altar. First go and be reconciled to your brother; then come and offer your gift" (Matthew 5:23, 24). Onesimus determined to make things right.

A perfect opportunity presented itself, for Tychicus, another of Paul's disciples, was planning to depart for Asia as bearer of the letters Paul was writing to the churches in Colosse and Laodicea. When Onesimus indicated an interest in returning, Paul included a brief letter to Philemon on his behalf, which a no less hostile critic than Ernest Renan called "a true little masterpiece of letter writing." The letter to Philemon was the most brilliantly nuanced, compelling letter of reconciliation in ancient history. It is a model of grace and charm. As such, it can be a great help to us all if we care to enhance our human relationships — especially those in the Body of Christ where we have special stake in each other's lives.

PAUL'S APPROACH TO RECONCILIATION: STRATEGY

In light of the magnitude of Paul's apostolic office, he could have assumed a Jimmy Cagney stance: "See here, Phil, this is Paul writing, the Boss Apostle. I've got this guy here, Onesimus, and he's converted and he's swell. So don't give him any trouble, see. If you do, I'll be over to see you. We have a little Latin saying here in Rome for people who don't go along with the program. It begins with *Jerkus*. You can fill in the rest. Now you wouldn't want that said about you, would you? So get with the program. So long, pal. Paulus Maximus." That was not Paul's way, nor is it ever the Christian way!

Notice Paul's tact. First, in verses 1 to 3 he cheerfully greeted Philemon and family by name, calling him "brother" (NASB) and his wife "sister" and their son a "fellow-soldier."

Second, he *sincerely* complimented Philemon in verses 4 to 7.

I always thank my God as I remember you in my prayers. (v. 4)

. . . because I hear about your faith in the Lord Jesus and your love for all the saints. (v. 5)

Your love has given me great joy and encouragement, because you, brother, have refreshed the hearts of the saints. (v. 7)

Next, in verses 8 and 9, Paul affirmed that his attitude was *not* dictatorial. He appealed to Philemon "on the basis of love," and love cannot be compelled. In addition, he mentioned that he was both aged and in jail, thus further appealing to Philemon's sympathy.

Lastly, as he got to his point in verses 10 and 11, Paul used some unexpected humor by making a pun on Onesimus's name, which meant "*useful*": "I appeal to you for my son Onesimus, who became my son while I was in chains. Formerly he was useless to you, but now he has become useful both to you and to me." There was undoubtedly a twinkle in Paul's eye, some playfulness. Paul was 145 words into his letter of 335 words, and this was the first mention of Onesimus, the main subject, and it was with a gracious lightness.

Paul's masterful approach to Philemon provides us with needed wisdom in dealing with our own relational problems. His example teaches us that fundamental to human reconciliation is taking the time to reflect on where people are: how they are feeling, how they perceive the problem, how they think we perceive them. We, above all people, ought to understand the secrets of human personality. Christian sensitivity is fundamental to reconciliation in human relationships.

Also, we must learn to choose our words carefully. Some people never give a compliment without a negative barb — "backhanded compliments." But Solomon says, "Like apples of gold in settings of silver is a word spoken in right circumstances" (Proverbs 25:11, NASB). Human reconciliation runs on loving tact, something every Christian should master regardless of personality or position.

Next, in his attempt to effect reconciliation, Paul described to Philemon his own *intimate* relationship with Onesimus. We see this in several key words prudently sprinkled throughout the letter. They are powerful, emotive nouns: *"son," "heart,"* and *"brother."* In verse 10 he said, "I appeal to you for my son Onesimus, who became my son while I was in chains." Paul describes Onesimus as his *child*, thus calling to mind one of the most precious and intimate of human relationships. Paul was bonded to Onesimus.

Paul reached for an equally strong expression in verse 12 when he said, "I am sending him — who is my very heart — back to you." The Greek word for "heart" is not the normal *kardia*, from which we get such words as *cardiac*, but an entirely different word which includes the idea of the feelings and compassion. Paul says, "I am sending you part of myself. That is how I feel about Onesimus."

Lastly, in verse 16 Paul used another emotive term in describing him as "a dear brother." The apostle could hardly be more forceful. *Onesimus was his child, his heart, his brother!* From this we learn an indispensable canon for building relationships: reconciliation and its cousins — intimacy, closeness, and fellowship — thrive when believers are able to express their true feelings. We think that others know how we feel when, in fact, they have not the slightest idea. If Paul had said he loved Onesimus, it would have indicated *something* of how he felt. But his choice of language left no doubt in Philemon's mind. This was a great step toward reconciliation.

Next, we observe briefly that Paul's approach was *positive*, as we see in verse 21 where he said to Philemon, "Confident of your obedience, I write to you, knowing that you will do even more than I ask." Paul believed in Philemon, and thus he expected good things to happen. I once heard George Sweeting say that optimism is when an eighty-five-year-old man marries a thirty-five-year-old woman and they move into a five-bedroom house next to a grade school! Here Paul was optimistic, and he expected good things to happen.

Paul let Philemon know that he believed in him. And Paul's positive faith did more for Philemon than a thousand queries and doubts could ever do. Faced with a tough relational situation? Pray and believe God for the best. You will be pleasantly surprised with the result.

In the same positive vein, in verses 15 and 16 Paul tantalized Philemon with the potential soul-satisfying relationship that awaited him and Onesimus: "Perhaps the reason he was separated from you for a little while was that you might have him back for good—no longer as a slave, but better than a slave, as a dear brother. He is very dear to me but even dearer to you, both as a man and as a brother in the Lord."

Onesimus was a double brother to Philemon—in the flesh and in the Lord. This is something of what Abraham Lincoln had in mind when he answered Thaddeus Stevens, who was demanding destruction of the enemy at the end of the Civil War. "Mr. Stevens," said Lincoln, "do I not destroy my enemy when I make him my friend?" Reconciliation makes our enemy our friend, perhaps even our intimate.

Finally note Paul's promise to pay all expenses for Onesimus, coupled with the assertion that Philemon "owed" him. "If he has done you any wrong or owes you anything, charge it to me. I, Paul, am writing this with my own hand. I will pay it back—not to mention that you owe me your very self. I do wish, brother, that I may have some benefit from you in the Lord; refresh my heart in Christ" (vv. 18-20). At this point Paul actually took the pen from his secretary and wrote the equivalent of a first-century IOU with his own hand. He put his "money where his mouth was." Indeed, according to Roman law he was liable to Philemon for the loss of work suffered[5]—not that he thought Philemon would really try to collect. Here again Paul's humor sparkled with another pun, for in verse 20 the word translated "benefit" had the same root as "Onesimus." He is saying, "Onesimus is your benefit or profit. So now, Philemon, you be my Onesimus, my benefit."

PAUL'S APPROACH TO RECONCILIATION: SUCCESS

Putting it all together: Consider Paul's gentle, artful tact with its cheerful greeting, his sincere compliments to Philemon, his loving attitude, his playful puns, and then Paul's description of his bond with his *child*, his *heart*, his *brother*. He really let Philemon know how he felt about Onesimus. Next came his positive expectation regarding Philemon's actions.

> *High Heaven rejects the lore,*
> *Of nicely calculated less and more.*[6]

Then came his tantalizing presentation of what would happen if they were reconciled, and finally his absurd offer to pay if necessary, along with the humorous reminder that Philemon "owed" him. Who could resist this, especially when it was read to the whole church (v. 2) while Philemon and Onesimus stood before them?

Surely forgiveness flowed! There was undoubtedly repeated embracing and kissing, Onesimus's repeated confessions, and Philemon's constant response, "That is enough, my dear brother!" As the church watched, there was constant praising of God.

Was this the end of the story? Surely not. Onesimus and Philemon went on to lead even more productive lives for Christ. Many believe that Philemon, in deference to Paul's expressed desire to have Onesimus back (vv. 13, 14, 20), returned him to Paul in Rome, where he further developed into a great man of God. The historical evidence is most suggestive of this. Fifty years later when Ignatius, one of the great Christian martyrs, was being transported from Antioch to Rome to be executed, he wrote letters to certain churches. In writing to Ephesus he praised their Bishop Onesimus, even making the *same* Pauline pun on his name! It appears likely that Onesimus, the runaway slave, had become, with the passing of years, the great Bishop of Ephesus.[7] This is one of the great stories of the gospel and of the Church — a jewel in her crown.

Think of what God did to secure Onesimus's reconciliation. Paul alluded to it in verse 15: "Perhaps the reason he was separated from you for a little while was that you might have him back for good." Paul recognized that Philemon's whole story was ultimately woven by God's hand. Onesimus's crime and flight were made to become, by God's grace, part of the plan for bringing Onesimus to himself — much as Joseph's being sold into Egypt by his brothers eventually brought their salvation. The more we study the story, the more we see that it transcends "chance." Onesimus fled the length of the world to escape his master and lose himself in the bowels of Rome, only to meet the very man to whom his master owed his spiritual life — and thus found spiritual life himself! How he must have marveled at God's tapestry.

The most confused, twisted life can ultimately come to be seen as a marvelous tapestry of God's grace. The evil that you did, or has been done to you, can be turned into the very thing that brings you to Christ. Onesimus is indeed "profitable," for from his life we learn the anatomy of reconciliation.

Soli Deo Gloria!

Notes

CHAPTER ONE: THE CELEBRATION OF THE CHURCH

1. Ralph P. Martin, *Colossians and Philemon*, The New Century Bible (London: Oliphants, Marshall, Morgan & Scott, 1978), pp. 18, 19. Dr. Martin says:

> In the Colossian church we appear to be in touch with a meeting-place where the free-thinking Judaism of the dispersion and the speculative ideas of Greek mystery-religion are in close contact. Out of this interchange and fusion comes a syncretism, which is both theologically novel (bringing Christ into a hierarchy and a system) and ethically conditioned (advocating a rigorous discipline and an ecstatic visionary reward). On both counts, in Paul's eyes, it is a deadly danger to the incipient church.

2. Alexander Maclaren, *The Epistles of St. Paul to the Colossians and Philemon*, The Expositor's Bible (New York: A. C. Armstrong, 1903), p. 17.
3. Martin, *Colossians and Philemon*, p. 46.
4. Peter T. O'Brien, *Colossians, Philemon*, Word Biblical Commentary, Volume 44 (Waco, TX: Word, 1982), p. 5.
5. John I. Durham, *Proclamation and Presence: Old Testament Essays in Honour of Gwynne Henton Davies* (Atlanta: John Knox Press, 1970), pp. 275-277, observes that in two-thirds of the instances of *shalom* in the Old Testament it is the result of the presence of God.
6. Eduard Schweizer, *The Letter to the Colossians*, trans. Andrew Chester (Minneapolis: Augsburg, 1982), p. 30.
7. Martin, *Colossians and Philemon*, p. 47 where he lists as examples 1 Thessalonians 1:3; 5:8; Romans 5:1-5; Galatians 5:5, 6; Ephesians 1:15, 18; 4:2-5; Hebrews 6:10-12; 10:22-24; 1 Peter 3:8, 21, 22; and Barnabas i:4; xi:8; Polycarp iii:2, 3.
8. R. C. Lucas, *Fullness and Freedom* (Downers Grove, IL: InterVarsity, 1980), p. 27.
9. Warren Wiersbe, *Be Complete* (Wheaton, IL: Victor, 1981), p. 24.
10. Charles Colson, *Born Again* (Old Tappan, NJ: Revell [Chosen Books], 1976), pp. 338, 339.
11. Eduard Lohse, *Colossians and Philemon*, trans. William R. Poehlmann and Robert J. Karris (Philadelphia: Fortress, 1971), p. 17, says:

> "Faith" and "love" are the hallmarks of the Christian life of the community, but "hope" refers to the content of the message which the community heard and accepted. This hope makes them capable of remaining firm in faith and practicing love to all the saints.

12. C. S. Lewis, *The Weight of Glory* (Grand Rapids, MI: Eerdmans, 1965), pp. 1, 2.

CHAPTER TWO: THE PRAYER FOR THE CHURCH

1. Lois Neely, *Come Up to This Mountain* (Wheaton, IL: Tyndale, 1980), p. 65.
2. F. F. Bruce and E. K. Simpson, *Commentary on the Epistles to the Ephesians and the Colossians* (Grand Rapids, MI. Eerdmans, 1957), p. 185. Bruce quotes Bieltmann, which is here reproduced.
3. Eduard Lohse, *Colossians and Philemon* (Philadelphia: Fortress, 1971), p. 25 says:

   He has been making constant and earnest prayer for them, similar to 1 Thess. 1:2; 2:13; Rom. 1:9; and Eph. 1:15. This is also indicated by the use of both "to pray" . . . and "to ask." This prayer is made to God with great intensity so that he may grant it.

4. Warren Wiersbe, *Be Complete* (Wheaton, IL: Victor, 1981), p. 35.
5. Harry Blamires, *The Christian Mind* (London: S. P. C. K., 1963), p. 43 says:

   . . . the Christian mind — a mind trained, informed, equipped to handle data of secular controversy within a framework of reference which is constructed of Christian presuppositions. The Christian mind is the prerequisite of Christian action.

6. Lohse, *Colossians and Philemon*, p. 30.
7. Ralph P. Martin, *Colossians and Philemon*, The New Century Bible (London: Oliphants, Marshall & Scott, 1978), p. 53.
8. Wiersbe, *Be Complete*, p. 43.
9. C. S. Lewis, *The Weight of Glory* (Grand Rapids, MI: Eerdmans, 1965), p. 13.
10. Peter T. O'Brien, *Colossians, Philemon*, Word Biblical Commentary, Volume 44 (Waco, TX: Word, 1982), p. 27, which refers to Josephus, *Antiquities*, 9.235 where the same word is used of Tiglath-pileser's removal of the Transjordanian tribes to his own kingdom.
11. Bruce and Simpson, *Commentary on the Epistles to the Ephesians and the Colossians*, p. 190 where Bruce says:

    It appears that Paul tends to distinguish these two aspects of the heavenly kingdom by reserving the commoner expression "the kingdom of God" for its future consummation, while designating its present phase by some such term as "the kingdom of Christ." We may compare his language in 1 Cor. 15:24, where Christ, after reigning until all things are put under His feet, delivers the kingdom "to God, even the Father"; Christ's mediatorial sovereignty then gives place to the eternal dominion of God.

CHAPTER THREE: THE PREEMINENT CHRIST

1. Warren Wiersbe, *Be Complete* (Wheaton, IL: Victor, 1981), pp. 52, 53.
2. William Barclay, *The Letters to the Philippians, Colossians, and Thessalonians* (Philadelphia: Westminster, 1959), p. 142.
3. Peter T. O'Brien, *Colossians, Philemon*, Word Biblical Commentary, Volume 44 (Waco, TX: Word, 1982), p. 43.
4. Ralph P. Martin, *Colossians and Philemon*, The New Century Bible (London: Oliphants, Marshall & Scott, 1978), p. 57 where he says:

   The really significant point to observe, however, is that in ancient thought *eikon* was believed not only to be a plaster representation of the object so portrayed, but was thought in some way to participate in the substance of the object it symbolized. 'Image is not to be understood as a magnitude which is alien to the reality and present only in the consciousness. It has a share in the reality. Indeed, it is the reality.' (H. Klienknecht, TDNT ii, p. 389). Thus Christ as God's image means that he is not a copy of God, 'like him'; he is the objectivization of God in human life, the 'projection' of God on the canvas of our humanity and the embodiment of the divine in the world of men.

5. Phillip Edgecumbe Hughes, *A Commentary on the Epistle to the Hebrews* (Grand Rapids, MI: Eerdmans, 1977), p. 41.
6. Eduard Lohse, *Colossians and Philemon* (Philadelphia: Fortress, 1971), p. 50.
7. O'Brien, *Colossians, Philemon*, p. 46.
8. *Ibid.*, p. 47.
9. H. Dermot McDonald, *Commentary on Colossians and Philemon* (Waco, TX: Word, 1980), p. 49.
10. From *The Collected Poems of Joseph Mary Plunket*, The Talbot Press, Dublin, as quoted in *The Interpreter's Bible*, Volume II, ed. George Arthur Buttrick (New York: Abingdon Press, n.d.), p. 166.

CHAPTER FOUR: THE SUPREME RECONCILIATION

1. Walter Lord, *A Night to Remember* (New York: Holt, Rinehart and Winston, 1976), pp. 70, 71.
2. F. F. Bruce and E. K. Simpson, *Commentary on the Epistles to the Ephesians and the Colossians* (Grand Rapids, MI: Eerdmans, 1957), pp. 206, 207.
3. William R. Nicholson, *Colossians — Oneness with Christ* (Grand Rapids, MI: Kregel, 1973), p. 90.
4. Clarence E. Macartney, *Macartney's Illustrations* (New York: Abingdon, 1946), p. 297.
5. Peter T. O'Brien, *Colossians and Philemon*, Word Biblical Commentary, Volume 44 (Waco, TX: Word, 1982), p. 66.
6. Arnold Dallimore, *George Whitefield*, Volume I (Westchester, IL: Crossway Books), p. 132.
7. R. C. Sproul, *The Holiness of God* (Wheaton, IL: Tyndale, 1985), p. 214.
8. O'Brien, *Colossians and Philemon*, p. 69.
9. Clyde S. Fant, Jr. and William M. Pinson., eds., *20 Centuries of Great Preaching*, Volume 6 (Waco, TX: Word), pp. 312, 313.

CHAPTER FIVE: THE SUPREME MINISTRY

1. R. C. Sproul, *Tabletalk*, April 1985, Volume 9, Number 2, p. 12.
2. John R. W. Stott, *Between Two Worlds* (Grand Rapids, MI: Eerdmans, 1982), pp. 22, 23.
3. Warren Wiersbe, *Walking with the Giants* (Grand Rapids, MI: Baker, 1979), p. 269.
4. Stott, *Between Two Worlds*, p. 43.
5. Peter T. O'Brien, *Colossians, Philemon*, Word Biblical Commentary, Volume 44 (Waco, TX: Word, 1982), p. 75.
6. *Ibid.*, pp. 78-81.
7. Wiersbe, *Walking with the Giants*, pp. 56, 57.
8. Gail MacDonald, *High Call, High Privilege* (Wheaton, IL: Tyndale, 1984), p. 86.
9. O'Brien, *Colossians, Philemon*, p. 90.
10. F. F. Bruce and E. K. Simpson, *Commentary on the Epistles to the Ephesians and the Colossians* (Grand Rapids, MI: Eerdmans, 1957), p. 221.
11. Ralph P. Martin, *Colossians and Philemon*, The New Century Bible (London: Oliphants, Marshall & Scott, 1978), p. 73.

12. G. Campbell Morgan, *The Westminster Pulpit*, Volumes 3, 4 (Old Tappan, NJ: Revell, n.d.), p. 160.
13. Maxie Dunnam, *Galatians, Ephesians, Philippians, Colossians, Philemon*, The Communicator's Commentary (Waco, TX: Word, 1982), pp. 363, 364.

CHAPTER SIX: THE SUPREME CONCERN

1. John R. W. Stott, *Between Two Worlds* (Grand Rapids, MI; Eerdmans, 1982), p. 285.
2. Clarence Edward Macartney, *Preaching Without Notes* (Grand Rapids, MI: Baker, 1976), p. 183.
3. W. E. Vine, *An Expository Dictionary of New Testament Words* (Old Tappan, NJ: Revell, 1966), p. 226.
4. Lyle W. Dorsett and Marjorie Lamp Mead, eds., *C. S. Lewis Letters to Children* (New York: Macmillan, 1985), p. 111.
5. F. F. Bruce and E. K. Simpson, *Commentary on the Epistles to the Ephesians and the Colossians* (Grand Rapids, MI: Eerdmans, 1957), p. 223.
6. Alexander Maclaren, *The Epistles of St. Paul to the Colossians and Philemon*, The Expositor's Bible (New York: A. C. Armstrong, 1903), pp. 165, 166.
7. Timothy Dwight, "I Love Thy Kingdom, Lord," 1800.

CHAPTER SEVEN: THE SUPREME CHARGE

1. Peter T. O'Brien, *Colossians, Philemon*, Word Biblical Commentary, Volume 44 (Waco, TX: Word, 1982), p. 106.
2. *The Annals of America*, Volume 17, "1950-1960, Cold War in Nuclear Age," 1968, p. 395.
3. Quoted by Ernest C. Reisinger, *Today's Evangelism: Its Message and Method* (Phillipsburg, NJ: Craig Press, 1982).
4. Hugh Evan Hopkins, *Charles Simeon of Cambridge* (Grand Rapids, MI: Eerdmans, 1977), p. 28.
5. R. C. Lucas, *Fullness and Freedom* (Downers Grove, IL: InterVarsity Press, 1980), p. 92.
6. Alexander Maclaren, *The Epistles of St. Paul to the Colossians and Philemon*, The Expositor's Bible (New York: A. C. Armstong, 1903), pp. 183, 184.

CHAPTER EIGHT: THE SAFEGUARD AGAINST SEDUCTION

1. Donald Grey Barnhouse, *Let Me Illustrate* (Old Tappan, NJ: Revell, 1967), p. 86.
2. F. F. Bruce and E. K. Simpson, *Commentary on the Epistles to the Ephesians and the Colossians* (Grand Rapids, MI: Eerdmans, 1957), p. 230.
3. Edwin Newman, *Strictly Speaking* (New York: Warner Books, 1977), pp. 171, 172.
4. *The Arizona Republic*, January 7, 1986, p. A-2.
5. Bruce and Simpson, *Commentary on the Epistles to the Ephesians and the Colossians*, p. 230.
6. Peter T. O'Brien, *Colosslans, Philemon*, Word Biblical Commentary, Volume 44 (Waco, TX: Word, 1982), p. 110.
7. *Ibid.*
8. Bruce and Simpson, *Commentary on the Epistles to the Ephesians and the Colossians*, p. 232.
9. O'Brien, *Colossians, Philemon*, p. 111.
10. R. E. O. White, *In Him the Fullness* (Old Tappan, NJ: Revell, 1973), p. 83.

11. Alexander Maclaren, *The Epistles of St. Paul to Colossians and Philemon*, The Expositor's Bible (New York: A. C. Armstrong, 1903), p. 198.

CHAPTER NINE: THE FULLNESS IN CHRIST

1. F. F. Bruce and E. K. Simpson, *Commentary on the Epistles to the Ephesians and the Colossians* (Grand Rapids, MI: Eerdmans, 1957), p. 234 where Bruce says:

   This "circumcision of Christ" is not primarily His circumcision as a Jewish infant of eight days old (Luke 2:21); it is rather his crucifixion, "the putting off the body of flesh," of which literal circumcision was at best a token anticipation.

2. Peter T. O'Brien, *Colossians, Philemon*, Word Biblical Commentary, Volume 44 (Waco, TX: Word, 1982), p. 118.
3. *Ibid.*, p. 116.
4. *Ibid.*, p. 119.
5. Plutarch, *The Lives of the Noble Grecians and Romans* (New York: The Modern Library, n.d.), pp. 340-342.
6. *Ibid.*

CHAPTER TEN: THE GUARDING OF YOUR TREASURE

1. Adapted from Joy Davidman, *Smoke on the Mountain* (Philadelphia: Westminster Press, 1953), p. 13.
2. James S. Hewett, ed., *Parables, Etc.*, Volume 6, Number. 1, March 1986, p. 1.
3. F. F. Bruce and E. K. Simpson, *Commentary on the Epistles to the Ephesians and the Colossians* (Grand Rapids, MI: Eerdmans, 1957), p. 250.
4. C. S. Lewis, *The Weight of Glory* (Grand Rapids, MI: Eerdmans, 1965), pp. 61-63.
5. R. E. O. White, *In Him the Fullness* (Old Tappan, NJ: Revell, 1973), pp. 90, 91.
6. Bruce and Simpson, *Commentary on the Epistles to the Ephesians and the Colossians*, p. 256.

CHAPTER ELEVEN: THE SEEKING OF THINGS ABOVE

1. F. F. Bruce and E. K. Simpson, *Commentary on the Epistles to the Ephesians and the Colossians* (Grand Rapids, MI: Eerdmans, 1957), p. 258, quoting *Weimar Ansgabe*, XXIII, p. 131.
2. Wesley H. Hager, *Conquering* (Grand Rapids, MI: Eerdmans, 1965), p. 16.
3. *Ibid.*, p. 15.
4. Os Guinness, *The Gravedigger Files* (Downers Grove, IL: InterVarsity Press), p. 132, quoting Frank S. Mead, *Handbook of Denominations* (Nashville: Abingdon, 1970), p. 217.

CHAPTER TWELVE: THE PUTTING OFF, PUTTING ON (I)

1. Warren Wiersbe, *Be Complete* (Wheaton, IL: Victor, 1981), p 103.
2. William Barclay, *The Letters to the Philippians, Colossians and Thessalonians* (Philadelphia: Westminster, 1959), p. 181.
3. Alexander Maclaren, *The Epistles of St. Paul to the Colossians and Philemon*, The Expositor's Bible (New York: A. C. Armstrong, 1903), p. 275.
4. William Barclay, *A New Testament Wordbook* (New York: Harper, n.d.), pp. 97-99.

5. Clarence E. Macartney, *Macartney's Illustrations* (New York: Abingdon, 1946), pp. 377, 378.
6. Maclaren, *The Epistles of St. Paul to the Colossians and Philemon*, p. 287.
7. Tertullian, *Apology*, 39.

CHAPTER THIRTEEN: THE PUTTING OFF, PUTTING ON (II)

1. Peter T. O'Brien, *Colossians, Philemon*, Word Biblical Commentary, Volume 44 (Waco, TX: Word, 1982), p. 199.
2. William Barclay, *The Letters to the Philippians, Colossians, and Thessalonians* (Philadelphia: Westminster, 1959), p 188.
3. John Perkins, *Let Justice Roll Down* (Ventura, CA: Regal, 1983), p. 203.
4. Barclay, *The Letters to the Philippians, Colossians, and Thessalonians*, pp. 188, 189.
5. F. W. Boreham, *The Heavenly Octave* (Grand Rapids, MI: Baker, 1978), p. 12.
6. *Ibid.*, p. 17.
7. *Daily Bread.*
8. Barclay, *A New Testament Wordbook*, pp. 103, 104.
9. R. E. O. White, *In Him the Fullness* (Old Tappan, NJ: Revell, 1973), p. 113.
10. Perkins, *Let Justice Roll Down*, pp. 162-166.
11. *Ibid.*, pp. 205, 206.
12. F. F. Bruce and E. K. Simpson, *Commentary on the Epistles to the Ephesians and the Colossians* (Grand Rapids, MI: Eerdmans, 1957), p. 281.

CHAPTER FOURTEEN: THE FULLNESS OF HIS PEACE, WORD, AND NAME

1. F. F. Bruce and E. K. Simpson, *Commentary on the Epistles to the Ephesians and the Colossians* (Grand Rapids, MI: Eerdmans, 1957), p. 281.
2. *Ibid.*, p. 284.

CHAPTER FIFTEEN: THE CHRISTIAN FAMILY (I)

1. Michael R. Tucker, *Live Confidently* (Wheaton, IL: Tyndale, 1976), p. 61.
2. William Barclay, *The Letters to the Philippians, Colossians, and Thessalonians* (Philadelphia: Westminster, 1959), pp. 192, 193.
3. Peter T. O'Brien, *Colossians, Philemon*, Word Biblical Commentary, Volume 44 (Waco, TX: Word, 1982), pp. 218, 219.
4. F. F. Bruce and E. K. Simpson, *Commentary on the Epistles to the Ephesians and the Colossians* (Grand Rapids, MI: Eerdmans, 1957), pp. 289, 290:

This phrase has a thoroughly stoic ring about it; but the injunction ceases to be stoic when Paul baptizes it into Christ by adding the words, "in the Lord." By treating the relation between the sexes in the context, Paul (contrary to much popular opinion) places essential dignity of women in general and of wives in particular on an unshakable foundation.

5. *Ibid.*, p. 289.
6. Eduard Lohse, *Colossians and Philemon* (Philadelphia: Fortress, 1971), p. 158, note 28: "Pre-Christian antiquity knew of the terms 'to love/love' . . . but in the Hellenistic world these terms do not occur in rules for the household."
7. Richard Seizer, *Mortal Lessons: Notes on the Art of Surgery* (New York: Simon and Schuster, 1976), pp. 45, 46.
8. Charles Swindoll, *Think It Over*, "Love Without a Net," a publication of the First Evangelical Free Church of Fullerton, California.

CHAPTER SIXTEEN: THE CHRISTIAN FAMILY (II)

1. James Dobson, *Hide or Seek* (Old Tappan, NJ: Revell, 1974), pp. 9, 11.
2. Karl Barth and Carl Zuckmayer, *A Late Friendship*, trans. Geoffrey Bromiley (Grand Rapids, MI: Eerdmans, 1982), p. 47.
3. Dobson, *Hide or Seek*, pp. 82, 83.
4. In Hebrews 1:23 the word *fathers (pateron)* means "parents" in the context and is translated "parents" in many translations. Nevertheless, the specific nature of the three pairs of injunctions in 3:18 – 4:1 would argue for "fathers" here.
5. Peter T. O'Brien, *Colossians, Philemon*, Word Biblical Commentary, Volume 44 (Waco, TX: Word, 1982), p. 225.
6. William Barclay, *The Letters to the Philippians, Colossians, and Thessalonians* (Philadelphia: Westminster, 1959), p. 195.

CHAPTER SEVENTEEN: THE CHRISTIAN FAMILY (III)

1. William Barclay, *The Letters to the Galatians and Ephesians* (Philadelphia: Westminster, 1958), pp. 212-214.
2. *Ibid.*
3. William MacDonald, *Ephesians, the Mystery of the Church* (Carol Stream, IL: Harold Shaw, 1968), p. 229.
4. Peter T. O'Brien, *Colossians, Philemon*, Word Biblical Commentary, Volume 44 (Waco, TX: Word, 1982), p. 229.
5. Humphrey House., ed., *Gerard Manley Hopkins, The Notebooks and Papers* (New York: Oxford, 1937), pp. 304, 305.
6. Alexander Maclaren, *The Epistles of St. Paul to the Colossians and Philemon*, The Expositor's Bible (New York: A. C. Armstrong, 1903), p. 352.
7. R. E. O. White, *In Him the Fullness* (Old Tappan, NJ: Revell, 1973), p. 127.

CHAPTER EIGHTEEN: THE FULLNESS IN COMMUNICATION

1. Thomas R. Kelly, *A Testament of Devotion* (New York: Harper, 1941), p. 35.
2. Brother Lawrence, *The Practice of the Presence of God* (Old Tappan, NJ: Revell, 1958), pp. 30, 31.
3. R. C. Sproul, *The Holiness of God* (Wheaton, IL: Tyndale, 1985), p. 54.
4. Michael D. Aeschliman, *The Restitution of Man* (Grand Rapids, MI: Eerdmans, 1983), p. 5.
5. John R. W. Stott, *Between Two Worlds* (Grand Rapids, MI: Eerdmans, 1982), p. 128.
6. Joseph Bayly, *I Love to Tell the Story* (Elgin, IL: David C. Cook, 1978), p. 36.
7. *Tabletalk*, Volume 10, Number 4, August 1986, p. 7.

CHAPTER NINETEEN: THE FULLNESS IN FELLOWSHIP (I)

1. A. W. Tozer, *The Pursuit of God* (Wheaton, IL:, Tyndale, 1982), pp. 119-123.
2. From the Department of Field Services, National Association of Evangelicals, January/February 1986 letter.
3. Lane T. Dennis, ed., *Letters of Francis A. Schaeffer* (Westchester, IL: Crossway Books, 1985), p. 108.

CHAPTER TWENTY: THE FULLNESS IN FELLOWSHIP (II)

1. Allen Emery, *A Turtle on a Fencepost* (Waco, TX: Word, 1979), pp. 75-78.
2. Warren Wiersbe, *Be Complete* (Wheaton, IL: Victor, 1981), p. 147.
3. Phillips Brooks, *The Influence of Jesus* (London: H. R. Allenson, 1875), p. 191.

CHAPTER TWENTY-ONE: THE FULLNESS OF PAUL'S HEART

1. Peter T. O'Brien, *Colossians, Philemon*, Word Biblical Commentary, Volume 44 (Waco, TX: Word, 1982), p. 257, where he says:

   The Epistles of the New Testament were from the first intended to be read aloud in the Christian assembly (showing that they ranked equally with the Old Testament), a point which is attested in one of Paul's earliest letters where he uses strong language in commanding that his letters be read aloud to all the brethren (I Thessalonians 5:17 . . .).

2. Alexander Maclaren, *The Epistles of St. Paul to the Colossians and Philemon*, The Expositor's Bible (New York: A. C. Armstrong, 1903), p. 411.

CHAPTER TWENTY-TWO: THE RECONCILING WISDOM

1. Andrew W. Blackwood, *Evangelical Sermons of Our Day* (New York: Harper and Bros., 1959), p. 338.
2. *Ibid*, p. 337.
3. H. Dermot McDonald, *Commentary on Colossians and Philemon* (Waco, TX: Word, 1980), p. 173, where he says:

   He has his own testimony to the sheer mercy of God. And if he already knows the content of Paul's letter, he will speak with thanksgiving to the Father who has qualified him to share in the inheritance of the saints in light, for his experience of deliverance (Colossians 1:12-14).

4. Charles Colson, *Who Speaks for God?* (Westchester, IL: Crossway Books, 1985), p. 153.
5. Ralph P. Martin, *Colossians and Philemon,* The New Century Bible (London: Oliphants, Marshall & Scott, 1978), p. 167, where he says:

   The underlying assumption is that Paul knows the law by which a person harbouring a runaway slave was liable to the owner for the loss of work involved in the slave's defection, see Preiss, loc. cit., p. 35. Oxrhynchus papyrus 1422 contains a notice that persons who gave shelter to escaped slaves were to be held accountable in law and could be prosecuted by the slaves' master.

6. William Wordsworth, *Ecclesiastical Sonnets*, Part 3, 43.
7. William Barclay, *The Letters to Timothy, Titus and Philemon*, pp. 315, 316.

Scripture Index

General Index

Taylor, Hudson, 138
Thankfulness, 16, 63, 64, 113
Transformation, example of Onesismus, 144-146
Trench, Archbishop, 102
Turkey, 14
Tychicus, 142-144

Walk,
knowledgeable, 25
Paul's prayer for Colossian walk, 21-27
powerful, 25, 26
thankful walk, 27, 28

worthy, 24, 25
Wesley, Charles, 112
Wesley, John, 24, 25, 49, 55, 112
White, R. E. O., 109
Whitefield, George, 48, 51
Whyte, Alexander, 44
Wiersbe, Warren, 23
Word of God,
and fathers, 126, 127
dwelling in believers, 111, 112
preaching of, 47
study of, 55, 111
Wycliffe, John, 43

About the Book Jacket

The design of the book jacket brings together the talents of four Christian artists. The design centers around the beautiful banner created by artist Marge Gieser. The banner is more than eight feet tall and was displayed in College Church throughout Pastor Hughes' series of sermons on Colossians and Philemon. It is photographed here on the jacket at about one-twentieth of its original size.

Concerning the symbolism used in the banner for *Colossians and Philemon* Marge Gieser writes:

> Christ, who has triumphed thru the cross, calls the church out of the dominion of darkness, to surrender to the divine call to a new life in Christ who is the head of all rule and authority.
>
> Colossians gives a prominent place to angelic orders as custodians of human destiny.

The other artists contributing their talents to the creation of the jacket were: Bill Koechling, photography; Paul Higdon, typography; Mark Schramm, overall design and art direction.